Quick and Easy Holiday Costumes

Quick and Easy

illustrated by Carolyn Bentley

Lothrop, Lee & Shepard Company

Holiday Costumes

written by Vivienne Eisner

A Division of William Morrow & Company, Inc. ☆ New York

1 2 3 4 5 6 7 8 9 10

Library of Congress Cataloging in Publication Data
Eisner, Vivienne.
    Quick and easy holiday costumes.
    SUMMARY: Describes how to make almost instantly more than five dozen
costumes for twenty-three holidays with inexpensive and easily available tools and
materials.
    1. Costume—Juvenile literature. [1. Costume. 2. Handicraft] I. Bentley,
Carolyn. II. Title.
TT633.E38   646.4′7   77-21987
ISBN 0-688-41809-0   ISBN 0-688-51809-5 lib. bdg.

Contents

Introduction

Wearing a costume is one of the best ways to celebrate almost any holiday. Go to a Valentine's party as the Knave of Hearts. Dress up at home like the Ackward Bay Erson Pay. Be Columbus in a school play. Join a 4th of July parade as the Statue of Liberty. At a church or temple festival, be an Easter bunny or Chanukah dreydl.

In this book, there are more than five dozen costumes for you to make and wear for holidays all year round. In addition to traditional holidays, such as Thanksgiving and Halloween, special occasions like Martin Luther King's Birthday, Chinese New Year, Earth Day, Purim, and American Indian Day are also included. Costumes for historical figures, such as Sacagawea and Pilgrim Man, are as identical as possible to the kind of garments these people might have actually worn. Finally, there are even costumes to wear for birthday festivities.

But best of all, these costumes can be made in a flash from inexpensive and easily-available materials. There are no patterns, no sewing, and no complicated directions. With just tape, glue, staples, scissors, hole punch, and tape measure, you can put together all the costumes in this book. You might be surprised how many items from around the house (such as old sheets, clothespins, cotton balls, and paper towels) can

9

be used to make good-looking costumes. Even your own clothes can be used in costume-making.

When you make your costumes, remember that you can mix and match parts from one costume with those of another. For example, if you want to be a Snow King or Queen, use the tunic from the Valentine King or Queen of Hearts (make it white, instead of red) along with the crown from Queen Isabella's costume. And the five basic costumes described in this book make it possible for you to create costumes of your design by using the headband, tunic, sandwich sign, full skirt, and cape as a base. With this book as a guide, and your own imagination, there is no limit to the number of different, quick, and easy costumes you can make.

Tools and Materials

You probably already have most of the tools and materials needed for the costumes in this book. If not, all are inexpensive and easy to find. You can buy what you need at a drug, variety, stationery, grocery, or art supply store.

Tools
You will need the following tools for nearly every costume. You might like to keep them in a shoe box or other container, so they will be handy all year round.

cellophane tape, ½- or ¾-inch wide
stapler and staples
nontoxic white glue, such as Elmer's
cloth tape measure
ruler, yardstick, or other straight edge
sharp-pointed scissors
pencil
hole punch

Decorating Materials
Magic Markers, felt-tip pens, and crayons are used to draw various designs and decorations. Crayons and Magic Markers are also useful for coloring white paper, when colored paper is not available. Paint is not used in this book.

Masking tape and colored plastic tape are sometimes used to make stripes, such as on Uncle Sam's pants and Judah Maccabeus' tunic. Dried cereal, pasta, candies, and similar food items are used as jewels and other decorative trim. Finally, scrap box odds and ends, such as wrapping paper, foil, yarn, ribbon, and nature materials, can be used to add fancy touches to nearly every costume.

Materials From Around the House

Once you have made a few of the projects in this book, you will notice how many scraps and throw-aways can be recycled into handsome costumes. Begin by saving such things as string, yarn, egg cartons, cardboard tubes, seed catalogs, pie tins, and empty cereal boxes. Look around your house for other good costume-making materials. From the kitchen, look for aluminum foil, paper towels, plastic wrap, grocery bags, baggie ties, and plastic utensils. In the bathroom or medicine chest, gather cotton balls, cotton swabs, toilet paper, bobby pins, paper tissues, and bandaids. Raid your desk drawer for rubber bands, paper clips, gummed stars, plain white paper, safety pins, bulletin board pushpins, and paper fasteners. And don't forget to check the give-away or scrap box for a discarded sheet, pillowcase, blanket, T-shirt or socks.

Paper

There are many different kinds of paper that you can use for the costumes in this book. Although specific types, such as construction paper or cardboard, are often suggested, feel free to substitute another paper of similar thickness and color.

Construction paper comes in a handy, variety-color package. The 18-inch by 12-inch size is the most useful. Construction paper is good to have for headbands, sandwich signs, hats with brims, and costume accessories.

Brown grocery and shopping bag paper is valuable as stiff paper. Cut the bag open so you have one flat piece of paper. Smooth out the wrinkles with the palm of your hand, and you are ready to cut out the costume part needed.

Crepe paper is suggested for several of the costumes. It is soft, colorful, and, most important of all, stretchable. It is sold as a sheet, 2 yards long and 20 inches wide, and as a roll, 2 inches wide and 44 feet long. Both are inexpensive, and can be found in stationery, variety, and art supply stores.

When the costume directions call for a large piece of paper, use a roll of shelf or wrapping paper. Or fasten several smaller sheets of paper together with staples or tape.

Fire safety care must be taken at all times, no matter what material you are wearing. But when you use paper to make a costume, be especially careful to keep away from flames.

Cloth

Whenever possible, use scrap cloth for your costume-making. Old sheets, drapes, blankets, towels, or ready-to-be-thrown-away clothing can be put to good use. If you want to buy cloth of a special color or texture, get the least expensive cotton or acrylic cloth from a yard goods, variety, or department store. Cloth is usually 36 inches or 48 inches wide, so one or two yards will be more than enough for an entire costume.

Finally, a second-hand clothing or thrift shop is a good source for inexpensive material, larger-sized clothing, old T-shirts that you can cut up, jewelry, scarves, belts, and exotic costume items.

13

Five Basic Costumes

There are five basic costumes used throughout this book: headband, tunic, full skirt, cape, and sandwich sign. Once you know how to make each of these, costume-making is a snap.

Headband

The headband is a circle worn around the top of your head like a cap. In this book, it is often used as the base for making various hats, headdresses, and hair styles. You can also make a neckband, wristband, ankleband, or waistband in the same way—just measure around your neck, wrist, ankle, or waist (instead of around your head) for the length of the band.

To make the basic headband without crosspieces, first find your head size. Measure around the top of your head, so the top edge of the tape measure is about 1 inch above your eyebrows (Figure 1). Add 1 inch to this figure for the length of the head-

figure 1

band. Unless a different size is given in the costume directions, the width of the headband before it is folded is always 3 inches.

Mark the length and width on the paper or cloth suggested for the headband in the costume directions. Cut out the rectangle and fold in half, long sides together. Overlap the short ends 1 inch, and staple the circle closed.

The open edge or "groove" of the headband is to be worn at the top. After the decorations and crosspieces have been added, this side is stapled closed.

When crosspieces are needed, make each from a 10-inch long and 1-inch wide strip, using the same material as for the headband. Slide one short end of the strip into the groove of the headband and the other end into the groove on the opposite side. Staple to hold (Figure 2). For two crosspieces, lay the second strip on top the first so they form an "X" at the top. Attach to the headband in the same way as the first strip.

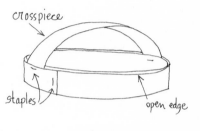

crosspiece

staples

open edge

figure 2

Tunic

The tunic is a loose-fitting, sleeveless garment that looks the same on both sides. It slips on over your head, and can be worn with or without a belt.

Make the tunic from the paper or fabric suggested in the directions for each cos-

figure 1

figure 2

tume. The width of the material is always the measurement across your chest from one underarm to the other (Figure 1), plus 4 inches.

The length of the material varies with the length of the tunic needed. To measure for the length, hold the small-numbered end of the tape measure at the top of your shoulder. Let the tape measure slide through your fingers until the end is next to your knee or ankle (whichever is specified for the costume). The measurement at your shoulder is the length of the tunic (Figure 2). Double this figure for the length of the material.

Mark the measurements on the material, and cut. Fold the long shape in half, short sides together. Bring the corners of only the fold edge together, and crease to mark the center of the fold.

Make a mark 3 inches on each side of the center crease (Figure 3). Then make a mark on the center crease, 1 inch from the fold edge. Cut out a curve joining these three points, cutting through both layers of material. This is the neck opening.

Slide the tunic on over your head, either side in front. If you need extra room for your head to slide through, make a cut straight down from the center of the neck

16

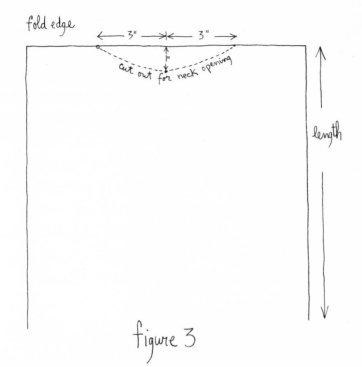

fold edge

← 3" →|← 3" →

cut out for neck opening

length

figure 3

opening at the front of the tunic. Make the cut long enough so you can take the tunic on and off without tearing it.

You can wear the tunic with the sides open or closed. To make closed sides, staple or tape the long, open edges together (right sides together, if you are using patterned fabric), leaving arm hole space on each side near the fold edge. Turn the material so the staples or tape are on the inside of the tunic.

Full Skirt

The full skirt has short pleats all around the waist for a gathered look.

Use the paper or fabric and color suggested in the costume directions. The width of the material is always double the measurement around your waist.

To measure for the length, hold the low-numbered end of the tape measure at your waist and let it slide through your fingers until the end is next to your knee or ankle (depending upon the costume directions). The figure at your waist is the length of the skirt and the length of the material.

Mark the material for the length and width, and cut it out. At the corner of one long side, make a short pleat about 1 inch deep. Staple closed (Figure 1). Continue pleating and stapling, making the folds about 1 inch apart, until the entire side is pleated. Be sure to fold all the pleats in the same direction.

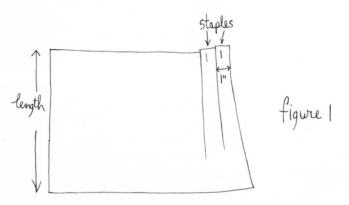

Wrap the pleated material around your waist, and make a mark on the pleated waistband where the sides overlap. Use this mark as a guide for taping the length of the skirt closed (Figure 2). Leave about 6 inches open near the waistband, so you can slide the skirt on and off.

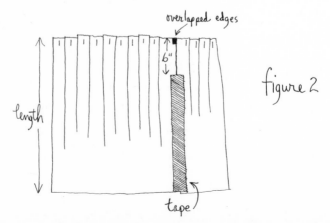

Cover the staples on the inside of the skirt with tape. Place small pieces of tape on the waistband where the edges overlap. Put the skirt on and fasten closed at the taped points with a safety pin. If you wish, cover the staples on the pleats with a scarf, sash, man's tie, or other belt.

Cape

The cape is a kind of armless coat made from paper or fabric. It is worn draped over your shoulders, and is held closed in front at the neck with a safety or jewelry pin, yarn or string ties, or tape.

Make the cape from the material suggested for each costume. The width of the cape material is always your chest measurement, plus 4 inches. To measure your chest, hold the small-numbered end of the tape measure in front of you while you wrap the tape measure around you and under both arms (Figure 1).

The way you measure for the length of the cape material is not always the same. Some capes are waist-length; some are knee-length; and some are ankle-length. Check the directions for each costume for the length you need. Then hold the small-numbered end of the tape measure at the top of your shoulders, and let the tape

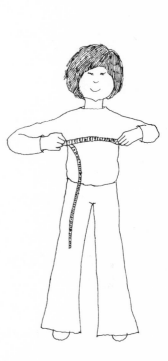

figure 1

19

figure 2

measure slide through your fingers until the end is next to your waist, knee, or ankle (Figure 2). The number at your shoulder is the length of the cape and of the cape material.

Mark the material for the proper measurements, and cut it out. Fold the material in half (right sides together, if you are using fabric), so the fold edge is the length of the cape. Lightly crease the fold, and open the material to lay flat. Fold the two lengthwise sides inward to meet at the creased center (see Figure 3).

On one of the open sides, mark points 3 inches from each corner (Figure 3). From the same corners, measure and mark

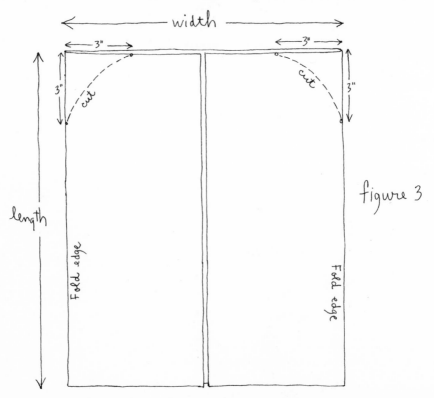

figure 3

two 3-inch points along the fold edges. Cut off the two corners in a curve, beginning and ending at the 3-inch marks.

Staple or tape the curved openings closed. Turn the cape material so the staples or tape are on the inside.

If you are using yarn or string ties, place a small piece of tape on each side of the center opening and near the top edge of the cape (Figure 4). Cut or punch a small hole through each piece of tape. Thread a short length of yarn or string through each hole, and knot or tape to hold.

You can vary the look of the cape by rounding the bottom corners at the front. Or you might like to trim each side in front, cutting on an angle upward from the bottom edge to make a narrower cape. Finally, you can make an extra-quick cape by pinning a towel, small rug, pillowcase, skirt, or table-cloth around your neck.

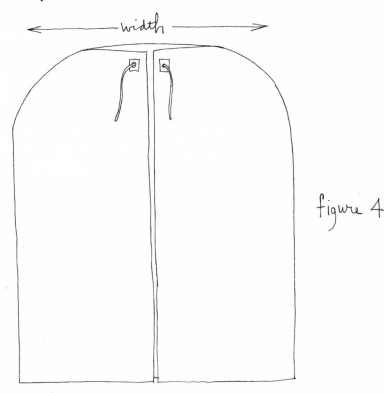

figure 4

Sandwich Sign

The sandwich sign is made from two identical shapes joined at the top edges by yarn or string ties. One piece hangs in front of you and one in back, so you are "sandwiched" in between.

Measure and draw the shape of the sandwich signs according to each costume's directions, and using the paper or fabric suggested. For a knee-length sign, measure from your armpit to your knee for the length and across your chest for the width of each piece. Many of the costumes leave the size of the sandwich sign up to you. Just remember that a sign that falls below your knees makes it a bit difficult to walk.

For the shoulder straps, make two marks 1 inch down from the top and 3 inches in from each side along one short edge of both pieces (Figure 1). Cover the marks with small pieces of tape. With closed, sharp-pointed scissors or a hole punch, poke a small hole through each taped section.

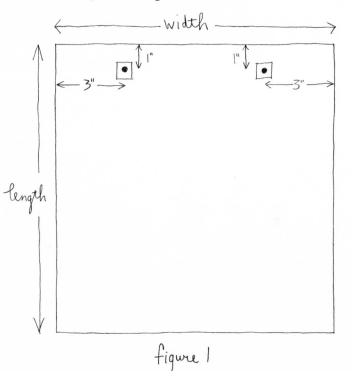

figure 1

Cut two pieces of string or yarn, each 15 inches long. Thread one piece through a hole in either sign. Tie a knot at the end of the string on the taped side of the sign. Repeat on the same sign for the second piece of string. Hold the two signs together with the taped holes on the outside. Thread the other end of one piece of string through the hole directly opposite on the second sign, and knot on the taped side to hold (Figure 2).

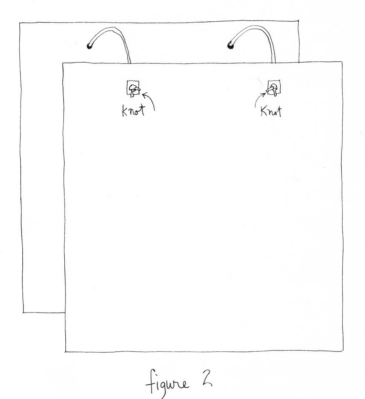

figure 2

Repeat for the remaining string end.

Hang the sign over your shoulders. If the sign is too long, adjust the shoulder straps by shortening each string at one end.

January

New Year's Day

Janus

The month of January gets its name from Janus, the Roman god of gates and doors. Janus was often shown with two faces, one looking forward and one looking backward.

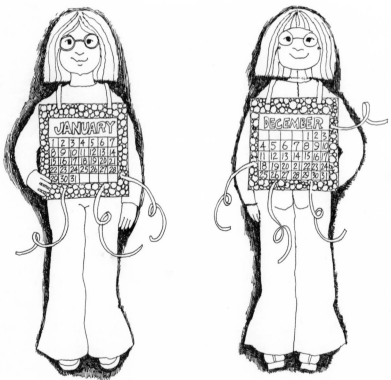

Wear
everyday clothes
cap (optional)

Make
☆ face mask
Make a life-size drawing of your face on a piece of paper. Cut it out. Place a small piece of tape at eye level and near the edge of both sides of the mask. With a hole punch, make a hole in each taped side. Thread a rubber band halfway through one hole. Tie to the mask by pulling the opposite end through the loop you have just formed (Figures 1a-c). Repeat for the second hole. Put the mask on the back of your head and slide the rubber bands over your ears to keep it in place.

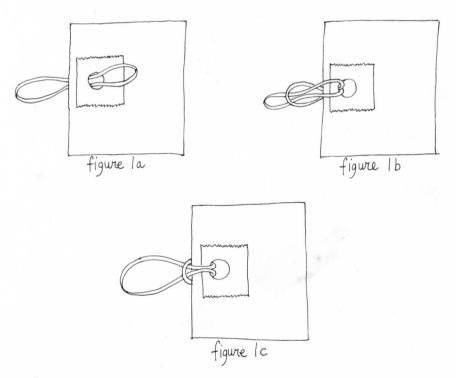

figure 1a

figure 1b

figure 1c

☆ sandwich sign

Make a sandwich sign (see p. 22) from any color construction paper. Decorate both sides with streamers, balloons, colorful scrap paper, foil, or any party materials you can find. You might fasten the December page of last year's calendar on the back sign and the January page of the new year's calendar on the front.

Cuckoo Clock

The clock sings out twelve "coo-coo" sounds to mark the close of the old year and the beginning of a new one.

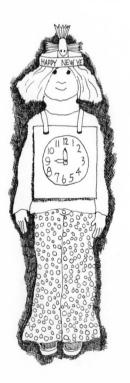

Wear
everyday clothes

Make
☆ New Year clock

Make a sandwich sign (see p. 22), at least 12 inches long and 12 inches wide, from any color construction paper. On the front sign, write the numbers 1 through 12 in a circle about 7 inches in diameter. Mark the center of the circle. Place the sign on a flat surface, and poke a hole through the center with closed, sharp-pointed scissors.

For the hands of the clock, cut two 1-inch wide paper strips, one 3 inches long and one 4 inches long. Cut one end of each strip to form a point. With a hole punch, poke a hole through both strips about ½ inch from the unpointed ends. Slide a paper fastener through the holes, and then through the hole in the center of the clock face. Close the fastener and tape the points to the back of the sign.

Decorate the back sign with a New Year's message, such as "Happy New Year, Welcome 19—." You might want to glue on streamers, confetti, balloons, or other party-type materials.

☆ bird headdress

Make a headband with one crosspiece (see p. 14). Write "Happy New Year" on the headband before stapling closed.

For the bird, cut a toilet paper tube in half, or use a 3-inch long section from a paper towel tube. Carefully poke a small hole in the center of this tube with closed, sharp-pointed scissors. Then cut a lengthwise slit ½ inch long. Repeat on the opposite side of the tube.

For the wings, cut two 4-inch squares from colorful paper. Magazine ads are good for this. Make a fan with narrow pleats from each square. Staple one end of each fan closed. Put the stapled ends into opposite slits in the tube.

For the tail feathers, pleat an 8-inch long and 10-inch wide piece of colorful paper from one long side to the other. Fold this pleated strip in half, short ends together (Figure 1). Slide the fold end through the tube until it sticks out slightly on the opposite side. The pleated paper flares out to form the tail.

figure 1

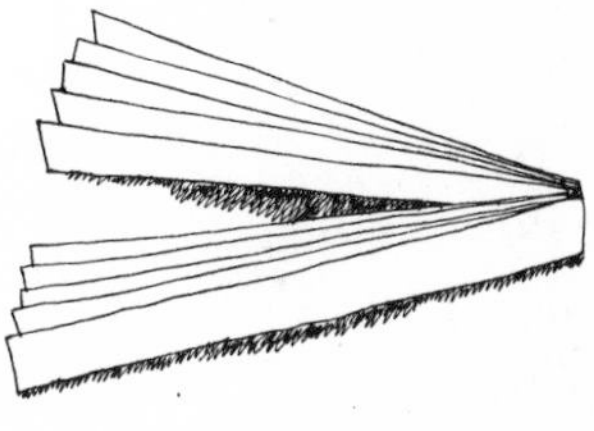

fold

For the beak, cut one divider from an

figure 2

egg carton. Glue it to the front end of the tube. Draw eyes on the beak piece with Magic Marker or felt-tip pen (Figure 2).

Place the bird on the crosspiece. Wrap tape around the bird and under the crosspiece several times to fasten securely.

Martin Luther King's Birthday

Martin Luther King, Jr.

Reverend Dr. Martin Luther King, Jr. was awarded the Nobel Peace Prize in 1964 for his leadership in helping Black people gain their civil rights. We celebrate his birthday by remembering his great work and dedication to peace.

Wear
long, dark pants
dark tie
long-sleeved, white shirt
dark shoes and socks

Make

☆ academic robe
Use black or any dark-colored cloth or paper to make an ankle-length cape (see p. 19).

☆ mortar board (academic hat)
Make a headband and one crosspiece (see p. 14) from construction paper, the same color as the robe.

From the same color construction paper, cut out an 8-inch square. Lay it on a flat surface, and poke a hole in the center with closed, sharp-pointed scissors.

Make a tassle from ten pieces of yarn, any color, each 8 inches long. Hold the yarn pieces together, ends even, and tape or baggie tie one end so the pieces stay together. Push the tied end of the tassle through the center hole in the square. Tape across the hole to keep the tassle in place. Glue the square to the crosspiece of the headband (see costume illustration).

☆ badge
Print "Nobel Peace Prize" on a small round paper plate or circle of paper. Staple or tape two pieces of ribbon or paper strips on the back. Tape or pin to the front of the robe.

☆ sign to carry
Print "I have a dream" on a piece of paper, about 9 inches long and 12 inches wide. Tape or glue a long stick or a flattened paper towel tube to the back of the sign.

Chinese New Year

Dragon

The ceremonial dragon always makes an appearance for the Chinese New Year celebration. In San Francisco's Chinatown, the dragon is one hundred and twenty-five feet long, and is made with silk and velvet. For this costume, however, only two people are needed, one for the head and one for the tail.

Wear (both)
long pants
long-sleeved T-shirt
knit gloves over socks (on your feet)

Make
☆ dragon mask
Open both ends of an empty, medium-sized cereal box. Cut four
or five points on the bottom flaps for the mouth. Pinch the
sides of the box together near the bottom flaps, and staple together on both sides and along the bottom flaps (Figure 1).

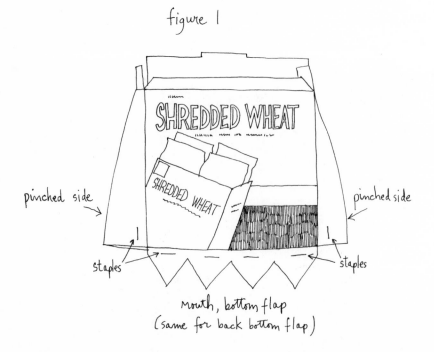

figure 1

pinched side

pinched side

SHREDDED WHEAT

SHREDDED WHEAT

staples

staples

mouth, bottom flap
(same for back bottom flap)

Press the sides of the box so the top end is a circular opening
large enough to fit around your face. Hold the top end over
your face at an angle so you are looking toward the mouth of

the mask (see costume illustration). Mark the front of the box for eye holes. Lay the box on a flat surface, and poke large eye holes with closed, sharp-pointed scissors.

Cut off the flaps from the top end of the box, except for the long, front flap. Cut two large triangles in the front flap for the ears. With a hole punch, make a hole in the center of each ear. Blow up two balloons only partway, and knot the necks. Put the balloon ends through the ear holes, and tape to the back of the ears to hold (Figure 2).

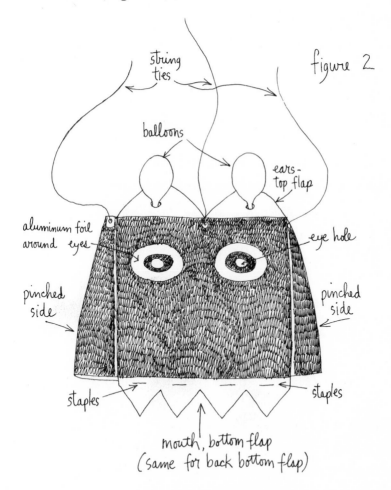

figure 2

string ties

balloons

ears - top flap

aluminum foil around eyes

eye hole

pinched side

pinched side

staples

staples

mouth, bottom flap
(same for back bottom flap)

Decorate the entire mask with scraps of colorful paper.

Cut two oblong shapes, about 2 inches long and 2½ inches wide, from aluminum foil. Fold in half, short sides together, and cut out a semicircle along the fold edge. Open, and glue or tape one oblong shape around each eye hole, shiny side outward.

At the top of the front and sides of the mask, punch a hole about 1 inch from the edge (see Figure 2). Thread string or yarn, about 15 inches long, through each hole and knot at one end to hold in place.

☆ dragon body

Cut two small holes, about 12 inches apart, near the center of the short edge of an old sheet. Thread string or yarn, about 15 inches long, through each hole. Knot each to hold in place.

Decorate one side of the sheet with paper chains (see *Monster*), styrofoam packing material, crayon, Magic Marker, or ribbons. Make noisemakers by stringing several foil plates together, and fastening the string to the sheet.

For the tail, staple or tape together at one end ten or more paper strips, each about 20 inches long and 3 inches wide. With a large safety pin or spring-type clothespin, attach the tail about 2 feet from the edge of the sheet opposite the string ties.

To Assemble

Put the mask over your face, and tie the side strings at the back of your head. The top string goes over your head, and is tied onto the back strings. You may need someone to help you tie this last string in place.

Put the sheet on your back and tie the sheet strings around

your neck. Your friend will climb under the sheet at the tail end, and bend over so the dragon has a lump-free back. For weaving in and out, have your friend hold on to your waist.

If you want to have a very long dragon, decorate another sheet and find another friend.

Festival Costume

Wear
long bathrobe
scarf or wide sash around your waist and
    tied in the back
white socks
fan, to carry

Make
☆ clogs
If you are not very heavy, you can wear egg-carton clogs. If you are, wear slippers or shoes.

Cut the divided section of two cardboard or styrofoam egg cartons to fit the length of your feet. Wad scrap paper into balls small enough to stuff inside the egg sections. Glue in place.

When you are ready to wear your clogs, place a sock-covered foot on top of one stuffed carton. Wrap tape around your foot and the carton near the toe end and

in the middle (see costume illustration). Repeat for the second clog. Walk slowly in true Chinese tradition, and avoid steps.

☆ headdress

Use a round, one-pound cereal box (such as an oatmeal or corn-meal container), without the lid and turned upside down. Or roll a piece of construction paper, about 14 inches long and 7 inches wide, into a tube. Overlap the short ends, and glue or tape closed.

Decorate the whole box or paper tube with wrapping paper scraps, colorful magazine pages, bits of aluminum foil, or any materials you prefer. You can also attach scraps of yarn, paper streamers, or paper flowers (see *Queen of the May*) to the headdress.

With closed, sharp-pointed scissors, poke a hole about 1 inch from the bottom edge of the box or tube. Make another hole on the opposite side. Cut two 15-inch long pieces of yarn or string. Thread each through one hole, and knot at one end to hold. Tie the headdress on your head.

February

St. Valentine's Day

Valentine Card

Extra Quick and Easy

Wear
party clothes

Make
☆ hat and sign
From red construction paper, make a heart-shaped sandwich sign (see p. 22). Decorate both sides with Valentine cards, lace-paper doilies, ribbon, candy, paper hearts, love poems and messages.

With a hole punch, make a hole on opposite sides of a large Valentine card. Thread a 15-inch long piece of ribbon, string, or yarn through each hole, and knot to hold. Place the card on your head like a hat, and tie the strings under your chin.

You can make a costume like this for Christmas, Chanukah, Easter, Purim, or any holiday when cards are exchanged.

37

King or Queen of Hearts

Wear

white or red T-shirt

white or red tights, or white or red long
   skirt or pants

slippers, or white or red socks

Make

☆ crown

Make a headband (see p. 14) from red
construction paper. Tape six white plastic
forks or spoons inside the groove of the
headband. Staple the groove closed. Decorate the headband with candy, paper
hearts, or cutouts from Valentine cards.

☆ cape

Use a large, white bath towel, or cut a
section from a white sheet which is as long
as the measurement from your shoulders
to the floor and twice as wide as your
shoulders.

Decorate this cape with hearts, each cut
from a 5-inch square of red paper (see illustration). Glue, tape, or staple each
heart to the long sides and one short side
of the cape. Wrap the plain short side
around your shoulders, and fasten closed
at the neck with a large safety pin.

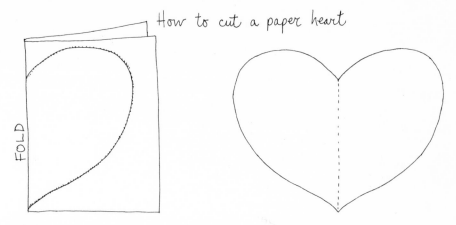

How to cut a paper heart

FOLD

☆ septer

Wad a 12-inch square of foil into a ball. Stick the pointed end of a long pencil into the ball. Glue or tape a Valentine card to the eraser end of the pencil.

Knave of Hearts

According to White Rabbit in Alice in Wonderland, it was the Knave of Hearts who "stole the tarts and took them clean away." Put some paper or real heart tarts on a plate to give to your friends on Valentine's Day.

Wear
red or white tights
long-sleeved, red or white T-shirt
knee-high boots (white, if possible), or
    red or white knee socks

39

Make

☆ tunic

From red paper or cloth, make a tunic (see p. 15) which is almost knee-length. Tie a white, 2-inch wide piece of cloth or crepe paper around your waist over the tunic. Cut out a large, white paper heart (see *King or Queen of Hearts*), and fasten it to the front of the tunic with tape or staples.

☆ hat

From red or white paper, cut out a rectangle 12 inches long and the width of half your head size, plus 2 inches (for measuring your head size, see the directions for the headband on p. 14).

Fold the rectangle in half, width sides together. Turn up the edges opposite the fold about 1½ inches (Figure 1). Cut a

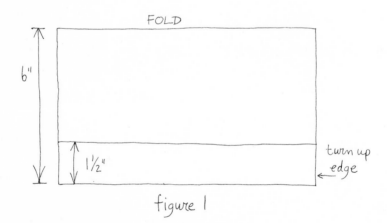

figure 1

rounded shape beginning and ending at the turned-up edges (Figure 2). Staple the rounded pieces together about 1 inch from the curved edge.

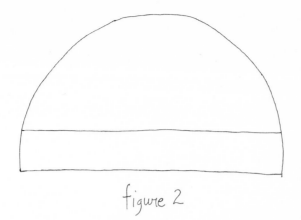

figure 2

Cut out four hearts, each from a 2-inch square of red paper. Staple the hearts to a drinking straw. Glue, tape, or staple the heart "feather" into the groove of the hat.

Abraham Lincoln's Birthday

Abraham Lincoln

Wear
dark pants
long-sleeved, white shirt
dark bow tie, or ribbon tie
dark shoes and socks

Make
☆ stovepipe hat
Make a headband (see p. 14) from black construction paper.
From black paper, cut a rectangle 8 inches wide and the same length as the headband. Staple this rectangle lengthwise to the headband to form the top of the hat. Overlap the short ends 1 inch, and staple or tape closed.

For the brim, fold a 12-inch square of black paper in half. Cut out a semicircle, beginning and ending at the fold. Open to form a circle (Figures 1a-b).

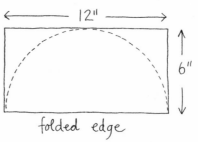

figure 1a

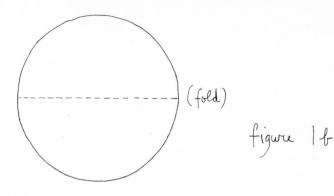

(fold)

figure 1 b

Place the top of the hat in the center of the circle. Trace the outline of the tube shape on the circle. Cut a straight line to the drawn circle, and cut it out. This forms an open ring (Figure 2).

Wrap the open ring around the head-band end of the top of the hat. Overlap the cut ends so the brim fits snugly, and staple closed (Figure 3). Attach the brim to the top of the hat with several pieces of tape to keep it in place.

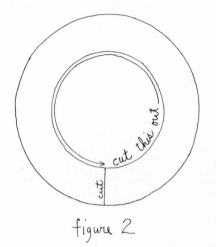

cut this out

cut

figure 2

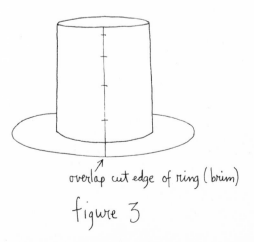

overlap cut edge of ring (brim)

figure 3

☆ beard

Cut a 3-inch wide piece of black paper so it is as long as your measurement from one ear under your lower lip to the other ear. Round off two corners on a long side to shape the beard.

Put a small piece of tape near the edge of the squared off corners. With a hole punch, make a hole through each taped part. Thread a rubber band halfway through each hole. Tie to the beard by pulling the opposite end through the loop you have just formed (Figures 4a-c). Slip the rubber bands over each ear to hold the beard in place.

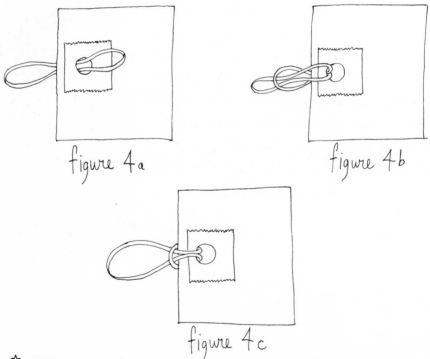

figure 4a

figure 4b

figure 4c

☆ cape

Use dark grey or black material from an old skirt, curtains, blanket, or fabric scraps to make a knee-length cape (see p. 19).

Mary Todd Lincoln

Extra Quick and Easy

Wear

long, full, dark-colored skirt

dark-colored blouse

dark shawl, scarf, or similar material, worn
around your shoulders and your waist

jewelry pin, to hold the scarf closed at the
front of your waist

dark shoes and socks

Make

☆ hat

With a hole punch, make holes on opposite sides of a large paper plate. Thread a
15-inch long piece of ribbon or string
through each hole, and knot at one end
to hold.

Cut out pictures of large flowers from
seed catalogs, paper towels, fabric, tissue
boxes, department store shopping bags,
or old greeting cards. Glue or staple to
the front of the hat. Put the plate on your
head, and tie the strings under your chin.

45

George Washington's Birthday

George Washington

Wear
long-sleeved, white shirt
dark pants
black or white knee socks, worn over your
    pant legs
large-sized vest
dark shoes

Make
☆ jabot (pleated frill at neck)
Make five or six pleats in a piece of white
paper or cloth, about 12 inches long and
6 inches wide, folding from one short side
to the other. Staple the pleats closed along
one edge. Cover the staples with a narrow
strip of paper or cloth glued along the
edge. Tape or pin the jabot to the front of
your shirt at the neck.

☆ wig
From white paper, make a headband with
two crosspieces (see p. 14).
   Cut about fifty white paper strips, each
10 inches long and 1½ inches wide. Curl
the ends of each strip by gently pulling
the blades of closed scissors over the

paper. You may want to do this two or three times to make a tight curl. Glue the uncurled part of each strip to the headband and crosspieces until they are hidden.

Make a ponytail from five white paper strips, each 6 inches long and 1½ inches wide. Staple the pieces together at one end and tie a ribbon or yarn bow around the staple. Staple the ponytail to the bottom edge of the headband at the back.

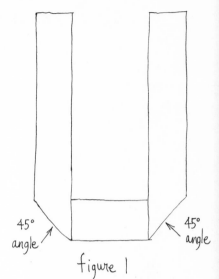

45° angle   45° angle

figure 1

☆ shoe buckles

For each buckle, use a piece of aluminum foil 12 inches long and 4 inches wide. Fold each piece three times along the long side to form a strip 12 inches long and ½ inch wide. Fold about 5 inches of each end so the strip forms a U-shape, with a base about 2 inches long (Figure 1). The bottom outside corners form angles of about 45 degrees. Fold the ends again so the U-shape becomes an open rectangle (Figure 2). Staple this last side closed. Shape the outside corners, if necessary, so all are 45-degree angles. Tape each buckle to the top of your shoes.

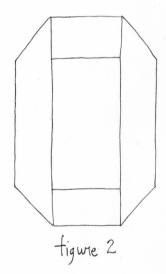

figure 2

☆ knee strings

Under each knee, tie a narrow piece of ribbon around your socks with the bow on the outside of your leg.

47

Martha Washington

Extra Quick and Easy

Wear

long-sleeved blouse

long, full skirt

lacy material, such as an old curtain or tablecloth, over the skirt. Tie it on around your waist with a pretty scarf, sash, or piece of ribbon.

lacy scarf around your shoulders, held closed at the front with a jewelry pin

party shoes and socks

dust ruffle shower cap, stuffed with crushed paper. Attach a jewelry pin to the front of the cap.

March

St. Patrick's Day

Leprechaun

According to Irish folklore, a leprechaun is a fairy shoe-maker who guards a gold treasure. When dressed as a lepre-chaun, you can sit cross-legged on a cushion and pretend to mend a shoe.

Wear
red or green pajamas, or long-sleeved, red
    or green T-shirt and tights
large, red or green knee socks (see
    "pointed slippers" below)
red or green ribbon around your waist

Make
☆ cap and beard
Cut a rectangle 16 inches long and 8 inches wide from red or green cloth or paper. Fold in half, short sides together. Staple all along one side next to the fold edge (Figure 1). Put a small piece of tape in each corner of the open side (see Figure 2). With a hole punch, make a hole

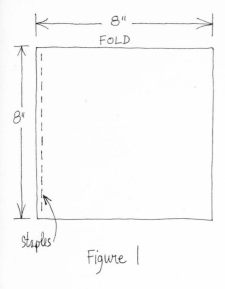

8"
FOLD
8"
Staples
Figure 1

through each taped part. Tie a 10-inch long narrow strip of white cloth, crepe paper, or ribbon through each hole. Knot to hold in place.

For the beard, spread two Teflon or copper pot scrubbers so they look like whiskers. Staple or tape to the cap strings near the holes (Figure 2). Leave enough room to tie the strings under your chin.

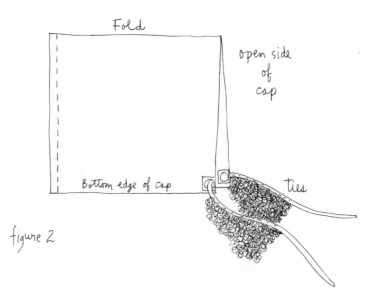

Fold
open side of cap
Bottom edge of cap
ties
figure 2

☆ pointed slippers
Stuff the toe end of each large sock with crushed newspaper. Put the sock on so the stuffed end is pointed upward, and the newspaper rests on the top of your foot.

50

Irish Country Lad

Wear

long-sleeved, white shirt or T-shirt
dark pants
knee-high boots, worn over the bottom of the pants
vest or sleeveless sweater
green bow tie, or green ribbon tied like a bow tie

Make

☆ hat

Make a headband (see p. 14) from green or black construction paper.

From the same colored paper, cut a rectangle 6 inches wide and the same length as the headband. Staple this shape to the headband along one long side. Overlap the short ends of the rectangle 1 inch at the headband edge and about 2 inches at the top. Staple or tape the short ends closed.

Use the same colored paper to make the brim. Cut out a 12-inch square, and fold it in half. Cut out a semicircle, beginning and ending at the fold. Open to form a circle (Figure 1).

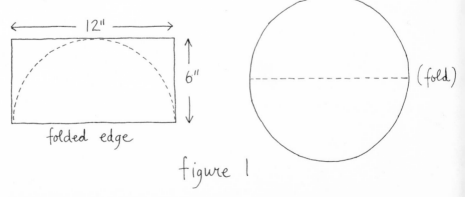

12"

6"

folded edge

(fold)

figure 1

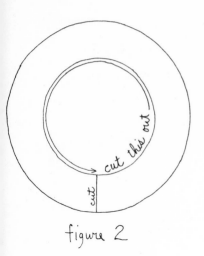

figure 2

Place the headband end of the hat in the center of the circle. Trace the outline of the tube shape on the circle with a pencil. Cut a straight line to the drawn circle, and cut it out. This forms an open ring (Figure 2).

Wrap the open ring around the headband end of the hat. Overlap the open ends so the brim fits snugly around the top of the hat. Staple the open ends closed. Fasten the brim to the top of the hat with several pieces of tape to keep it in place.

Tie a green ribbon around the hat, just above the brim. Cut out a green paper shamrock (Figure 3), and glue to the front of the hat.

figure 3

☆ pipe

Use one section cut from an egg carton. Poke a hole in the side with closed, sharp-pointed scissors. Slide the end of a straw into the hole, and tape to hold.

Irish Country Lass

Wear

long-sleeved, white blouse or T-shirt

two long, full skirts (The skirt on top is shorter than the one underneath. Tuck the hem under about 4 inches and tape, staple, or pin to hold.)

knee socks and school shoes

green shawl or scarf, worn around your shoulders or over your head

Make

☆ belt

Cut a 4-inch wide strip of black cloth or paper so its length is 1 inch less than your waist measurement. Tape all along the short ends of the strip. With a hole punch or closed, sharp-pointed scissors, make three equally-spaced holes through both taped ends. Put the belt around your waist, tape side inward, and lace with red or green yarn (Figure 1).

figure 1

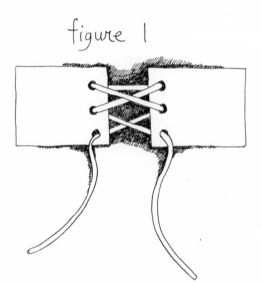

Purim

Purim is celebrated on the fourteenth day of the Hebrew month of Adar, which falls sometime in February or March. The merrymaking and festive air of this holiday is even carried into the synagogue, where the Megillah, *or Book of Esther, is read. This Biblical account describes how Queen Esther cleverly foiled the plot of Haman, a wicked minister to the King, to destroy all the Jews of Persia. Dressing up as the main characters in the Queen Esther story is one of the customs of this holiday.*

Queen Esther

Wear

bathing suit, leotard, or short-sleeved
   T-shirt and shorts
sandals or ballet slippers
necklaces, earrings, bracelets, ankle bracelets, pins, rings

Make

☆ headdress

Mold a piece of aluminum foil over your head so it fits like a cap or helmet. Tuck the edges under and shape so the cap forms a curved edge all around.

   Cut three circles, each 3 inches across, from purple, blue, or red paper. Decorate each circle with tiny pieces of tissue paper, gummed stars, dried beans or whatever you have that looks jewel-like. Staple one circle to the front of the headdress and one over each ear.

☆ skirt

Tie a silky scarf or a pretty belt around your waist. Collect at least six colorful, narrow scarves or men's ties (or fold head-scarves into narrow strips). Tape or pin to the scarf or belt around your waist. The more scarves you use, the fuller the skirt.

☆ cape (optional)

Use any see-through material, such as a section from an old cur-tain or a large chiffon scarf, large enough to reach from your shoulders to your waist. Wear like an oversized bib, and hold closed at the back of your neck with a jewelry pin.

Haman

During the reading of the Megillah, *mention of the villain Haman is followed by boos, foot-stomping, and twirling of* graggers *or noisemakers.*

Wear
long-sleeved, dark T-shirt
long, dark pants
sandals

Make

☆ tunic

Make an ankle-length tunic (see p. 15) from any dark-colored material (such as an old curtain, tablecloth, or blanket) or paper.

Use 2 yards of rope, twine, or 1-inch wide cloth to wrap around your waist. Center the rope at the back of your waist. Wrap it around your waist by crossing the ends in the front, the back, and in the front again. Tuck the ends under this belt, and bring them over your shoulders, forming an "X" on your chest (see costume illustration). Ask a friend to cross them on your back, and tuck them under the belt at your waist, as before. Bring the ends to the front and tie.

☆ hat

Make a headband with 1 crosspiece (see p. 14) from dark-colored paper.

Cut an 8-inch square from the same colored paper. Mark the center of one of the sides. Draw a line connecting this point to the two opposite corners (Figure 1). Cut out this triangular shape and staple, tape, or glue to the crosspiece. Wear the three-cornered hat with one of the points in front.

☆ beard

Cut a 5-inch wide piece of sandpaper so it is as long as your measurement from one ear under your lower lip to the other ear. Trim one long side into a curve to form the bottom edge of the beard. Cut

hat

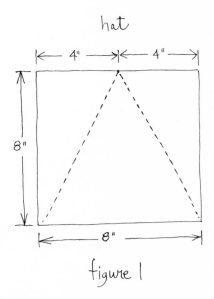

figure 1

57

3-inch long slits, ¼ to ½ inch apart, along this edge.

In each squared-off corner, place a small piece of tape. With a hole punch, poke a hole through each taped corner. Thread a rubber band halfway through each hole. Tie to the beard by pulling the opposite end through the loop you have just formed (Figures 2a-c). Slip the rubber bands over each ear to hold the beard in place.

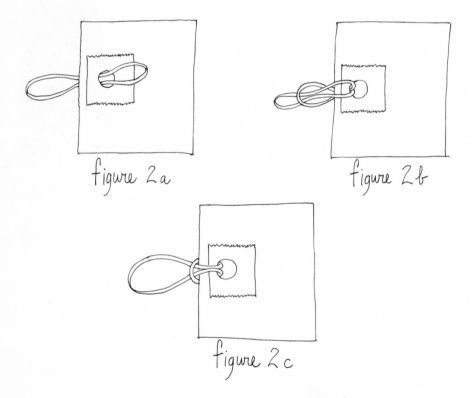

figure 2a

figure 2b

figure 2c

April

April Fool's Day

Mixed Up

Extra Quick and Easy

Wear
bunny costume (see *Easter*), and carry a
sign which says, "I am an elephant."

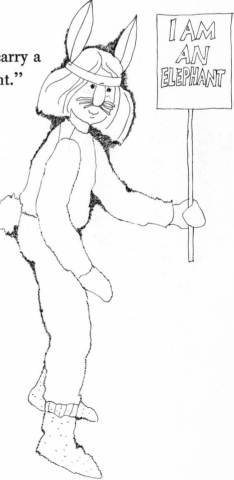

Ackward Bay Erson Pay

Wear forward
long pants
T-shirt
socks

Wear backward (see "To Assemble" below)
oversized jacket
tie
gloves
oversized socks
see-through scarf
baseball cap

Make
☆ mask
Measure around your head at eye level. Cut a 2-inch wide cloth or paper strip, any color, 1 inch longer than your head measurement. Overlap the short ends 1 inch, and staple the strip closed.

Put the band on over your head and mark it for eye holes. Remove the band, and cut out the marked places.

Cut out a life-size photograph of a face from a newspaper or magazine, or draw a face on a round paper plate. Glue the face onto the band directly opposite the eye holes.

To Assemble

Stuff the sleeves of the jacket with crushed newspaper, and pin a glove facing backward to each sleeve. Put on the tie and jacket on top your regular clothes so they face backward (Keep your arms loose inside the jacket—do not put them in the sleeves.) Ask a friend to help button the jacket closed. Stuff the toe end of the oversized socks with newspaper, and slide over your regular socks with your toes in the heel end. Drape the scarf over your head and face. Wear the mask over the scarf with the face at the back of your head. Put the baseball cap on with the visor shading the false face. When you walk, the Ackward Bay Erson Pay walks backward.

Easter

Easter Bunny

Wear

light-colored knit pajamas

pink or white socks over your hands and
feet

Make

☆ ears

Make a headband (see p. 14) from white
paper so that it fits low on your forehead.

Cut two ear shapes from pink or white
egg carton lids or from two pieces of white
posterboard, each 12 inches long and 3
inches wide. Crease the ears lengthwise
down the center. Staple one ear to each
side of the headband.

☆ nose and whiskers

Cut the toe end from a dark sock. Staple
to the bottom edge of the headband in between the ears, with the open end of the
sock facing inward (see costume illustration). Slide the headband onto your head,
and pull the sock so it covers your nose.

For whiskers, thread broom bristles, carpet thread, or stiff
twine through both sides of the lower edge of the sock nose. Or
staple baggie ties or pipe cleaners to the outside lower edge.

62

Bend the pointed ends inward, and cover the staples on the inside of the nose with tape.

☆ tail

Crush a half-page of newspaper into a ball and tape closed. Stretch a section of rolled cotton, about 6 inches square, over the newspaper ball to cover it. Tape in place. Attach the cotton tail to the back end of your pajamas with a safety pin or tape.

Easter Egg

Wear

everyday clothes

Make

☆ egg-shaped sign

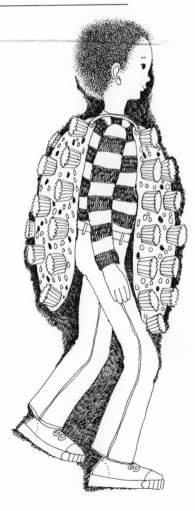

Cut four identical egg shapes from paper, making them as long as the measurement from your neck to your knees. Use either plain paper, such as grocery bag or brown mailing paper, or colorful construction or wrapping paper. Pair off these four pieces and, edges even, staple each pair together all around the edge leaving one long side open.

Make a sandwich sign (see p. 22) from these double-layered egg shapes.

Glue paper cupcake liners to the front and back of the sandwich sign. Arrange them in a colorful Easter egg design, cov-

63

ering as much of the signs as you wish. Cut jelly beans or other sticky Easter candy in half with kitchen shears. Use the sticky side of the candy like a glued edge, and press onto the sandwich signs to decorate the center of the cupcake liners, the border of the eggs, and wherever else you wish (see illustration).

Stuff each sign with crushed newspaper, sliding it through the open edge, until the two sides look like pillows. Staple the open sides closed.

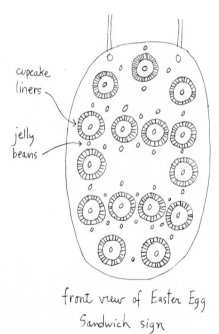

front view of Easter Egg
Sandwich sign

Earth Day and Arbor Day

Earth Day and Arbor Day remind us of the importance of conserving the earth's resources. Arbor Day and Earth Day celebrations vary from state to state, but usually happen sometime in the spring.

Fruit Tree

Extra Quick and Easy

Wear
long pants, brown or green if possible
long-sleeved T-shirt, brown or green if
    possible
sneakers
brown or green mittens or gloves (op-
    tional)

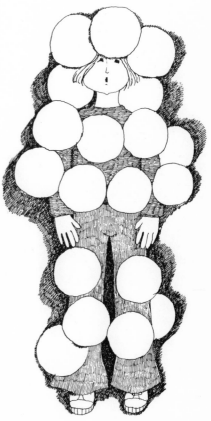

You need at least one dozen balloons. Choose the color according to the kind of tree you want to become. Use red balloons for an apple tree, orange balloons for an orange tree, yellow balloons for a lemon tree, green balloons for a lime tree, and so on.

Blow up the balloons and knot at the neck. Tie the balloons to string or yarn, long enough to tie around your waist,

chest, arms, legs, and head. Cover yourself from head to toe with balloons.

Mother or Father Nature

Wear
everyday clothes
carry a litter bag in one hand and a garden
    tool in the other

Make

☆ ecology sign

Make a sandwich sign (see p. 22) from brightly-colored posterboard.

Collage the front and back with things you have collected from nature. Glue on leaves, acorns, pebbles, shells, pine cones, grasses, seed pods, or flowers. You can also print your own ecology message, such as "Care for our Earth" or "Plant a Tree Today."

☆ headdress

Make a headband (see p. 14) from brown paper.

Gather five twigs, each about 6 inches long, or use five drinking straws or pipe cleaners. Cut out leaf shapes from paper, using a real-leaf pattern or the one on this page (Figure 1). Glue or tape five or more leaves to each twig. Tape the twigs inside the open edge of the headband (Figure 2). Staple the edge closed to keep the twigs in place.

figure 1

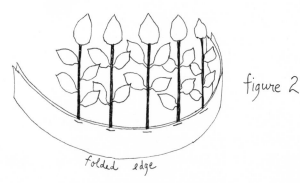

figure 2

folded edge

Johnny Appleseed

Extra Quick and Easy

No Arbor Day would be complete without mentioning Johnny Appleseed. According to legend, Johnny Appleseed wandered through the Ohio River Valley frontier planting apple seeds and seedling trees.

Wear

ragged, patched blue jeans, cut off below
the knees. (Pin the patches on, or use
adhesive tape and draw on stitch marks
with Magic Marker or felt-tip pen.)

ragged shirt

piece of rope tied to a belt loop on your
pants, one end in the front and one in
the back (or one suspender)

saucepan on your head

burlap bag or knapsack filled with seeds,
rice, or tiny pasta pieces

small book (Johnny Appleseed's Bible)
tucked in the top of your jeans

no shoes or socks

May

May Day

Queen of the May

May Day is an ancient holiday which might have begun as a New Year festival when prehistoric people celebrated the changing seasons. Later, in England, it became the custom to gather Hawthorn (May) blossoms along country lanes early in the morning on the first day of May. The blossoms were used to crown a pretty village girl Queen of the May.

Wear

bathing suit, or shorts and sleeveless
    T-shirt
sandals, ballet slippers, or barefeet

Make
☆ flower headdress

Make a headband (see p. 14) from white
or pastel-colored paper.

Make the flowers from white or pink
paper tissues. For each flower, cut one
section of a tissue in half widthwise. Unfold so the tissue lays flat. Pinch the two
long sides together and staple in the center (Figure 1). Bring two halves of a long

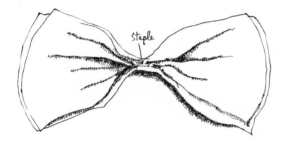

figure 1

edge together to form a fan, and staple to
hold (Figure 2). Repeat with the other two

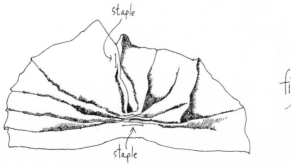

figure 2

halves to complete the flower (Figure 3).

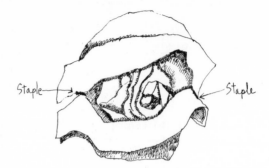

figure 3

Staple—   —Staple

Make at least six flowers and staple around the headband. You can make a flower necklace, wristbands, and ankle bracelets, too. Tape the tissue flower to ½-inch wide ribbon, long enough to tie around your neck, wrists, or ankles.

☆ tunic
Make an ankle-length tunic (see p. 15) from an old sheet, lacy curtain, or any pastel-colored or spring-print fabric. Large sheets of crepe paper, wrapping paper, paper tablecloths, or shelf paper can also be used. If you wish, decorate it with flower ads cut from magazines or seed catalogs.

☆ May basket
Tie a yarn or string handle to a small cardboard or plastic produce container, such as a berry or tomato basket (or use a

basket leftover from Easter). Line it with real or Easter-basket grass, crushed, green foil wrapping paper, or thin, green paper strips. Fill with real or homemade flowers.

Maypole

Ancient Maypoles were really large trees brought in from the forest. In the Middle Ages, English villages would compete with one another for the tallest Maypole. Dancing around the decorated Maypole was a popular custom.

Wear
leotard and tights, or pants and T-shirt
socks and sneakers

Make
☆ Maypole headdress
Make a headband and crosspiece (see p. 14) from colorful paper.

Poke a hole in the center of a large paper plate with closed, sharp-pointed scissors. Place a small piece of tape in the center of the top and underside of the crosspiece. With a hole punch, poke a hole through the taped section. Line up the holes of the paper plate and crosspiece, and fasten together with a paper fastener. Tape the points of the fastener to the underside of the crosspiece.

Cut streamers from crepe paper or ribbon which are as long as your measurement from head to toe. Use two or more colors, if possible. Staple the streamers to the paper plate, spacing them evenly around the edge and alternating colors.

☆ flower garland
Cut apart the twelve sections from an egg carton. Cut four, evenly-spaced slits in each section, going from the rim almost to the center. Bend the cut parts back to form the flower petals.

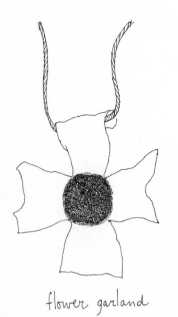

flower garland

Color the petals with Magic Marker, or cut out a flower picture from a seed catalog or magazine and glue in the center of the flower.

Cut a piece of yarn or string, about 24 inches long. Tape each flower to the yarn along the edge of one petal (see illustration). Space the flowers evenly to form a necklace or belt. Tie around your neck or waist.

Memorial Day

Memorial Day is a time to honor the millions of men and women who lost their lives during wartime. It is a day to march in a parade, and express hope for peace throughout the world.

Parade Costume

Wear
everyday clothes
black armband

Make
☆ headdress

Make a headband (see p. 14) from green paper.

Decorate it with paper tulips, buttercups, and poppies. Use red or purple paper for the tulips; yellow paper for the buttercups; and bright orange paper for the poppies. For each tulip, cut out a 5-inch wide circle; for each buttercup, a 3-inch wide circle; and for each poppy, a 4-inch wide circle. For each flower, fold the circle into quarters, and crease the fold edges. Open the circle and make a hole in the center with closed, sharp-pointed scissors.

Slide a cotton swab or short length of straw through the hole. Place your thumb

76

and forefinger on opposite sides of the circle, and pinch the paper near the center hole to bring up the sides. Continue pinching around the center hole until the circle forms a flower shape (Figure 1). Adjust the cotton swab to the right height to look like the inside of a flower, and staple in place near the center hole. Color the cotton tip with Magic Marker, if you wish.

Space the flowers evenly around the groove of the headband and glue in place. Staple the groove closed.

☆ sandwich sign

Make a sandwich sign (see p. 22) from red, white, or blue paper. Decorate with gummed stars, paper flowers (see headdress) stapled around the edges, and small American flags. Print "Remember May 30" on one or both sides.

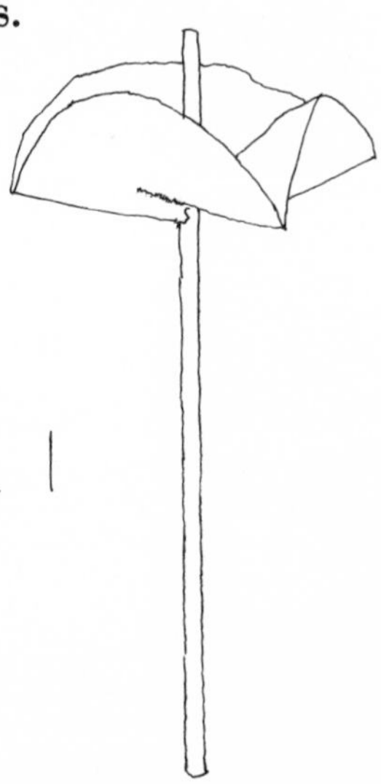

figure 1

Nurse

Wear

long-sleeved, white blouse or T-shirt

white stockings or tights

white shoes or sneakers

white skirt or long, white pants

oversized, dark blue skirt for a cape. Wrap the waist end around your shoulders, and pin closed at your neck.

Make

☆ cap

Make a headband (see p. 14) from white paper.

Cut a rectangle 11 inches long and 4 inches wide from white paper. Pleat the entire sheet working from one short side to the other. Staple the pleated piece to the front of the headband so the pleats run from top to bottom (see illustration).

Instead of a pleated sheet of paper, you might cut a section from white corrugated cardboard (such as the inside of a light bulb container) 6 inches long and 4 inches wide. Staple to the front of the headband along one long side.

☆ Red Cross nurse cap
Use an old white pillowcase or any similar-sized white cloth or paper. With red Magic Marker or crayon, draw a large red cross at the center of one long edge (or cut out a red cross and glue it to the case). Hold the pillowcase so the red cross is at the center of your forehead, and tie the short ends of the case at the back of your neck.

Marine

Wear
blue pants
short-sleeved, khaki-colored or light
    brown shirt
white belt
dark shoes

Make
☆ stripes and medals
pant stripes—Attach red tape or self-stick ribbon from the waist to the edge of the cuff on the side of each pant leg. If you don't have red tape or ribbon, use masking tape and color it with red Magic Marker.
shirt stripes—Attach narrow masking-tape officer stripes to both sleeves. These

79

are V-shapes turned upside down with slightly curved lines underneath (see costume illustration). Color them with blue Magic Marker.

shirt medals—Cut a 4-inch length of red or yellow ribbon or paper, about 1 inch wide. Tape a large coin or bus token to one end. Tape the other end a few inches below your shoulder on the left-hand side of your shirt front. Add as many medals as you wish, using smaller or larger coins.

☆ hat

Make a headband with one crosspiece (see p. 14) from white paper.

For the visor, cut a rectangle 6 inches long and 3 inches wide from black paper. Fold over one long side about 1 inch. Cut a curved edge on the other long side, beginning and ending at the fold (Figure 1). Crease the fold edge firmly, and staple or tape to the inside edge of the headband.

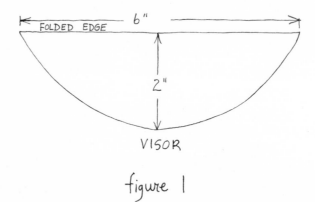

figure 1

Glue a white paper plate (or circle cut from white paper) to the crosspiece for the top of the hat.

June

Flag Day

Betsy Ross

Although many history experts doubt the story, Betsy Ross, a Philadelphia seamstress, is often described as our first flag-maker.

Wear

long skirt

long-sleeved blouse

apron

party shoes and socks

shawl or narrow scarf, pinned closed in the center of your waist
 with a jewelry pin

Make

☆ dust ruffle cap

Cut a 20-inch square from any light-colored cloth or crepe paper. Fold in half. Cut out a semicircle, beginning and ending at the fold edge. Open to form a circle.

With a hole punch, make holes about 1 inch apart and 1 inch from the edge all around the circle.

Cut a piece of ribbon or yarn 15 inches longer than your head size (see measuring instructions for the headband, p. 14). Thread the ribbon through one hole in the circle, leaving about 8 inches hanging loose. Weave the ribbon in and out of the holes, ending next to the hole where you began.

Put the cap on your head. Gently pull the ribbon, gathering the edge of the circle, until the cap fits snugly. Carefully remove the cap. Tie a knot in the ribbon to hold the ruffle, then tie a bow. Stuff the cap with crushed newspaper before you put it on again. Wear with the bow in the back or the front.

☆ 1777 flag

Cut a rectangle 20 inches long and 13 inches wide from red paper or fabric. Cut six strips of 1-inch wide white ribbon or tape, each 20 inches long, for the white flag stripes. Attach to the red paper so the white stripes are 1 inch from each long side and 1 inch apart (Figure 1).

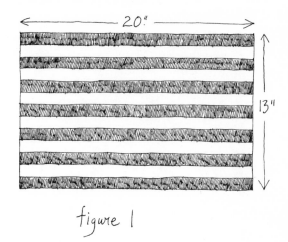

figure 1

Cut out a 7-inch square from blue paper or fabric.

Draw or cut out thirteen white stars (see *Uncle Sam*, p. 90, for how to draw a star), and glue in place in a large circle on the blue square. Tape, staple, or glue the blue square to the upper left corner of the striped paper (Figure 2).

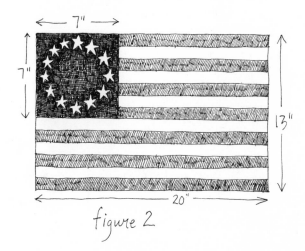

figure 2

All-Around Flag

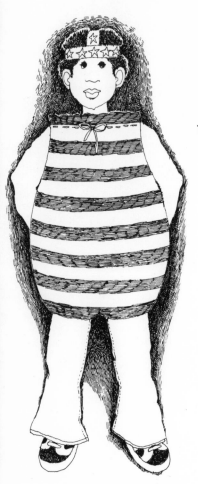

Wear

long-sleeved, white shirt
blue jeans or navy tights
red, white, or blue socks and sneakers

Make

☆ flag bag

Use a large, white pillowcase, or make one from a white sheet.

To make a case, fold the sheet in half. Cut out a double-thickness rectangle that is as long as the measurement from your neck to below your knees, and as wide as your shoulders. Do not cut the fold edge —it forms one of the short sides of the case. Staple or tape the long sides together (Figure 1). Turn so the staples or tape are on the inside of the case.

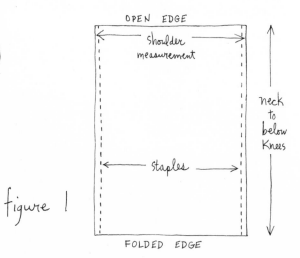

figure 1

On the short fold edge of the case, cut out two holes large enough for your legs to pass through. Cut out arm holes about 6 inches from the open end (see Figure 2). With sharp scissors, cut tiny slits 2 inches from the edge all around the open end of the case. Cut a piece of red or blue yarn, about 24 inches long, and weave it in and out of the slits. Leave enough yarn hanging loose from the first and last slits so you can tie the ends together later (Figure 2).

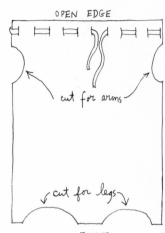

figure 2

With red Magic Marker or crayon, draw eight stripes running widthwise all around the case. Or tape wide masking tape colored with red Magic Marker (or red crepe paper strips) all around the case. Space the stripes so the eight red stripes are separated by six white stripes (see costume illustration).

Step into the bag. Stuff it full with crushed paper. Pull the yarn ties to gather the neck end. Tie closed.

☆ headdress

Make a headband and two crosspieces (see p. 14) from blue construction paper.

Use white gummed stars, or make them from white paper (see *Uncle Sam*, p. 90, for how to draw a star). Glue the stars to the headband and crosspieces, attaching fifty stars if possible.

July

4th of July

Statue of Liberty

The Statue of Liberty stands on Liberty Island in the New York Harbor, a gift from France as a symbol of friendship and liberty.

Wear
shorts and long-sleeved shirt
sandals

Make
☆ crown
Make a headband (see p. 14) from green construction paper.

Cut eight large points, all the same size, from two egg carton lids (Figure 1). Discard one point.

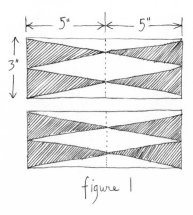

figure 1

Staple the points inside the open, front edge of the headband, spacing them equally in a semicircle. Staple the open edge closed. Bend the points forward to look like rays from the sun.

☆ torch

Make five, equally-spaced, 2-inch cuts along the rim of a large paper cup. Bend the flaps outward.

Cut a hole in the center of the bottom of the cup, large enough for a paper towel tube to pass through. Slide the paper towel tube through the cup hole, until it is several inches above the flaps. Glue the tube in place.

Crush a piece of flame-colored paper, and glue it to the top of the tube.

☆ draped garment

Cut or tape a piece of green sheet, lightweight blanket, crepe paper, tablecloth, or other fabric so it is 6 feet long and as wide as your measurement from neck to ankle.

Tape the corner of a short side to the front center of your shirt (Figure 2). Put the rest of the material under your left arm, across your back, under your right arm, and back to the front center. Pin securely to the taped corner (Figure 3).

figure 2

figure 3

87

Once pinned, you can remove the tape. Bring the top edge of the remaining material over your left shoulder so the bottom edge angles upward off the floor to about knee height (see costume illustration). Pin in place at your left shoulder with a large safety pin.

Uncle Sam

Uncle Sam's initials are "U.S." It took an Act of Congress in 1961 to make Uncle Sam officially a national symbol.

Wear

long-sleeved, white shirt or T-shirt

blue jeans

red, white, or blue socks

white sneakers

blue bow tie, or large bow made from blue cloth or crepe paper. Attach gummed stars, if you have them.

Make

☆ swallow-tailed coat

Use an oversized blue jacket. Tape the sleeves to fit your arm length. Turn the lower edge of each side of the jacket inward in a V-shaped fold, and tape to the inside lining (see costume illustration).

For the buttons, tape two bottle caps or coins to the back of the jacket at the waist and about 2 inches apart.

88

☆ hat

Make the top of the hat from white construction paper, 10 inches wide and 1 inch longer than your head size (see head-band, p. 14, for how to measure your head size). Draw red stripes, about 1 inch wide, with crayon or Magic Marker. Draw them widthwise on the paper, and about 1 inch apart (see Figure 3). Instead of drawing the stripes, you might use 1-inch wide red ribbon or masking tape colored red. Overlap the short sides of the striped rectangle 1 inch, and staple or tape the tube closed.

For the brim, fold a 12-inch square of white construction paper in half. Cut out a semicircle, beginning and ending at the fold edge. Open to form a circle. Put the top of the hat in the center of the circle. With a pencil, trace the outline of the edge of the tube onto the circle. Cut a straight line to the drawn circle. Then cut out the inner circle, forming an open ring (Figure 1). Slide the ring over the striped tube so it rests near one open end. Overlap the ends of the ring so it fits the tube snugly. Staple closed. Tape the brim to the hat in several places.

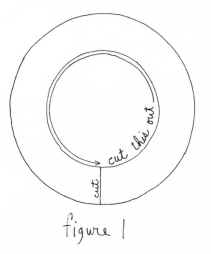

figure 1

Cut a 2-inch wide strip of blue paper, long enough to wrap around the hat just above the brim. Draw white stars (Figure 2) almost as wide as the strip along the entire length. Wrap

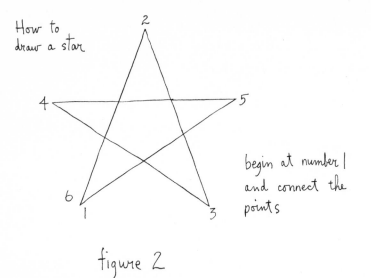

How to draw a star

begin at number 1 and connect the points

figure 2

the strip around the hat just above the brim (Figure 3) and staple or glue to the hat.

figure 3

☆ beard

Cut open an empty light bulb container (or use any corrugated container). Cut a section 4 inches long and 2 inches wide. Attach one short edge to your chin, white side facing outward, with flesh-colored bandaids.

☆ pant stripes
Attach four strips of masking tape, about 1 inch wide, from the waist to the cuff of each pant leg. Space the strips evenly, and color with red Magic Marker.

August

Birthday Celebration

Fortune Teller

Wear

colorful scarf, wrapped around your head
and tied at the back of your neck
long, full, colorful skirt or pants, tied at
the waist with a wide scarf or sash
brightly-colored blouse or T-shirt
colorful scarf or sash around your
shoulders
dangling earrings
bracelets and necklaces
slippers or sandals

Print fortunes on slips of paper. Here are
some fortune ideas:

A surprise awaits you.

A large, four-footed animal will become
your friend.

Someone you know will win a contest.

You will find something small, round,
and valuable.

You will get an unexpected present.

A special prize is yours, if you take a
chance.

A pleasant meeting will soon take place.

A new friend is just around the corner.

You will have an exciting adventure
soon.

A dark-haired person will tell you a
secret.

You will get something you have always wished for.

You will receive a mysterious note.

Let your guests draw these fortunes from a decorated box. Or read their fortunes from a "crystal ball" made by turning a fish bowl or other round, clear container upside down.

Birthday Present

Wear
whatever you want to

Make
☆ birthday package sign
Make a sandwich sign (see p. 22) from two large, rectangular pieces of posterboard or cardboard.

Staple, glue, or tape birthday wrapping paper onto the sides facing outward. Fasten ribbon on top the paper so the sign looks like a gift package. Glue on one or more ribbon bows. You can print "Happy Birthday to ——" on one side of the sign, or make a large birthday card from construction paper and tie it onto one of the shoulder straps of the sign.

☆ cake headdress
Make a headband and two crosspieces (see p. 14) from white paper.

Attach the bottom of a small, round or square, aluminum foil cake pan to the crosspieces with staples or tape.

Make the "cake" from newspaper or foil, crushed and shaped to fit inside the foil pan like a one-layer cake. Glue or tape to hold inside the pan. "Frost" the cake with paper tissues, tissue paper, paper napkins, or paper towels, any color you prefer. Use enough "frosting" to cover the newsprint or shiny silver of the "cake," and tape or glue to hold. You can make additional cake layers in the same way, gluing one on top of the other.

Decorate the top layer of the cake with real or pretend food. Use toothpicks to attach marshmallows, small soft candies, raisins, or other food. Do not use glue so you can eat your cake later. For non-food decorations, use bulletin board pushpins, gummed stars, fancy cocktail toothpicks, brads, and other colorful items that can be stuck directly into the cake to hold them in place. Attach a small toy or charm to the cake, if you wish (Figure 1).

figure 1

For a candle, peel the paper off an old crayon. Stick one end of the crayon into a small empty spool. Make a hole in the cake for the spool with closed, sharp-pointed scissors. Glue the spool into the hole.

September

American Indian Day

Tecumseh

There are many great Indian heroes and heroines. One of the most famous Indian leaders is Tecumseh. A Shawnee from what is now Ohio, he spent his lifetime travelling east of the Rocky Mountains from one tribe to another, trying to unite them against the white man.

Wear

tan or brown pants
tan or brown knee socks
long-sleeved, tan or brown T-shirt
moccasin slippers, ballet slippers, or
    heavy socks

Make

☆ headdress

From white paper, cut out eight feather shapes, each 8 inches long and with a 2-inch wide base. Make short slits along both long sides of the feathers to fringe. Staple a drinking straw or pipe cleaner about 6 inches long down the center of each feather. Color the tip of the feathers with red crayon or Magic Marker. Set aside three feathers for the peace pipe. Fold over the base of the remaining five feathers about 1 inch, so the flap is on the side opposite the straws.

Cut a strip 10 inches long and 1 inch wide from a grocery bag or other brown paper. Place the five feathers widthwise along the brown paper strip, spacing them evenly and beginning about 1 inch down from one short end. Straw side outward, staple each feather to the strip (Figure 1).

Hold the short end of the feathered strip to the back of your head, and attach

figure 1

97

the headdress to your hair with one or more bobby pins.

☆ bear claw necklace
Color ten spring-type clothespins with black Magic Marker. Clip all to a piece of string or yarn, long enough to tie around your neck.

☆ fringe
From a brown grocery bag or other brown paper or cloth, cut two 2-inch wide strips which are as long as the back of your knee socks. Fold each in half, long sides together. Unfold and cut slits as deep as the crease and as close together as possible along one long side of each strip.

Pull the knee socks over your pant legs. With masking tape, attach the uncut edge of the fringe to the back of each sock (Figure 2). Crease the strip along the center fold so the fringe stands away from the sock.

figure 2

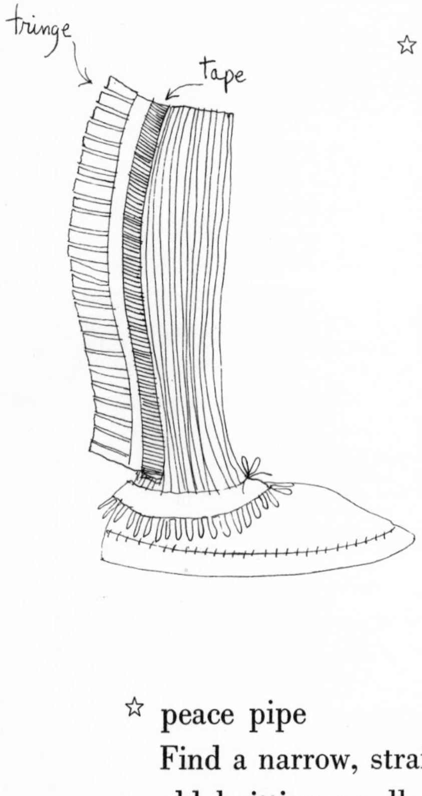

fringe

tape

☆ peace pipe
Find a narrow, straight stick about 15 inches long, or use an old knitting needle, kite stick, or balsa dowel. With closed, sharp-pointed scissors, carefully poke a hole in the side of a small, empty frozen juice can. Slide the stick into the hole and glue in place. Cover the can with brown paper or masking tape. Wrap masking tape around the stick to match the bowl of the

pipe. Tape three feathers (see headdress) to the stick near the can end.

Sacagawea

Sacagawea of the Wyoming Shoshone tribe was called the Bird Woman because she was alert and ran swiftly. Sacagawea was the first woman to cross the Rocky Mountains when she led the Lewis and Clark expedition to the Pacific Ocean.

Wear

long pants

long-sleeved T-shirt

knee socks

heavy white knee socks over your regular socks

doll to carry in the papoose holder on your back

unpatterned head scarf, tied under your chin

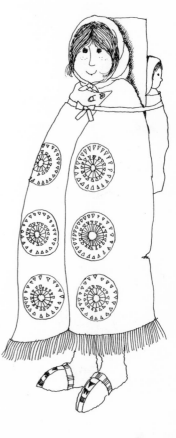

Make

☆ cape

Make an ankle-length cape (see p. 19) from tan burlap (available at hardware, department, or yard goods stores). Make the cape extra wide so you can wrap it around you like a large blanket.

Pull out the lengthwise strings along the bottom edge until you have fringe

about 2 inches long. Draw Shoshone designs on the front of the cape with Magic
Marker (Figure 1). Hold closed at your
neck with a large safety pin.

If you cannot find burlap, you can use
grocery bags cut open to lay flat and taped
together to form the size you need. Fringe
the bottom edge by cutting 2-inch slits as
close together as possible.

figure 1

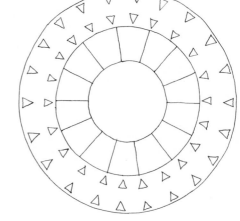

☆ moccasins

Attach masking-tape strips widthwise
across the top of each white sock, near the
center of your foot. Run another strip
from the center of the toe end of each sock
to the center of the crosswise masking tape
strip (Figure 2). Draw designs on the
tape with felt-tip pen or Magic Marker.

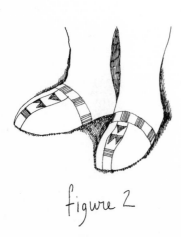

figure 2

100

☆ papoose holder

Cut a piece of cardboard or posterboard so it is 5 inches longer than your doll and as wide as your back.

Find a small paper bag which is large enough to hold your doll. If necessary, trim the top edge from a larger bag and fold in the sides so they are no wider than the cardboard. Place the bag flat against the cardboard so the bottom edges of both are even. Staple or tape the sides and bottom of the bag to the cardboard (see Figure 3).

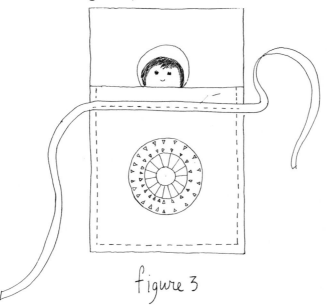

figure 3

Decorate the front of the bag with Shoshone designs drawn with crayon, Magic Marker, or colored pencils.

Cut a narrow strip of cloth or twine so it is 3 feet long. Center the strip about 2 inches from the top edge of the paper bag. Staple the strip to the bag all along the top edge (Figure 3). Place your doll in the bag.

With the paper bag on the outside, hold the cardboard on

101

your back over the cape, so the cloth or twine is even with your shoulders. Bring the ends of the cloth or twine to the front and tie.

Osceola

Osceola was the leader of a group of Seminole Indians in Florida who refused to surrender their homeland to the United States government and move to reservations in Oklahoma. Osceola's descendants still live in the Florida Everglades.

Wear
long-sleeved, brown or tan T-shirt
brown or tan pants
tan or white knee socks, worn over the pant legs
colorful scarf, wrapped like a turban around your head and tied at the back
colorful scarf or sash, tied around your waist over the tunic

Make
☆ headdress
Draw two large feathers on black construction paper. Each is 3 inches wide at the base and 10 inches long. Cut them out and make small cuts along both long edges to fringe. Tape the feathers to the head scarf so the points of the feathers point downward.

☆ tunic

Make a knee-length tunic (see p. 15) from colorful towels or sections of old sheet, bedspread, or blanket. Wear it over your T-shirt and pants.

☆ fetlocks (animal hair pieces)

You will need nine fetlocks: three for the waist sash, one for each wrist, and two for each legging.

For each fetlock, cut ten 5-inch pieces of white, tan, black, or brown yarn. Hold the ten pieces together, ends even, and wrap tape around one end.

Tape three fetlocks to the front of the sash at your waist. Tie three small bows made from ribbon or yarn, and glue over the tape. Tie a length of ribbon around the T-shirt at each wrist. Tape or glue one fetlock to each piece of ribbon.

☆ leggings

Wrap a colorful piece of cloth, 2 inches wide, around the top of each knee sock. Pin closed and pin to each sock. Tape two fetlocks to the side of the cloth wrapping. Tape masking tape down the front of each leg, and another strip across the toe end of each sock (Figure 1).

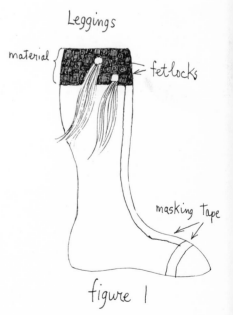

Leggings

material {

← fetlocks

masking tape

figure 1

☆ breast plate necklace

From an egg carton lid or any stiff paper, cut three semicircles, each 4 inches long and 2 inches wide. Cover each piece with aluminum foil.

103

Lay them flat, one under the other. Tape together with cellophane tape along both outside edges (see Figure 2). Turn over and tape to cover the sticky side of the first two strips.

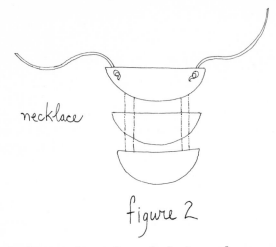

necklace

figure 2

With a hole punch, make a hole in each corner of the top foil piece. Cut two 15-inch long pieces of string or yarn. Thread one through each hole and knot to hold (Figure 2). Tie the necklace around your neck and, if possible, also wear two or three strands of your own beads.

October

Columbus Day

Christopher Columbus

Wear
long-sleeved, dark T-shirt
dark shorts
tights, any color
dark shoes or ankle-high boots

Make
☆ knee-length tunic
Make an extra-quick tunic from two dark towels. Staple or tape each towel so it is as wide as your measurement from shoulder to shoulder, and as long as your measurement from shoulder to knee.

Overlap the corners along one short side, and pin the towels together. Slip the towel tunic over your head and hold closed with a bright-colored scarf, man's tie, or sash around your waist.

☆ hat
Make a headband (see p. 14) from construction paper, any color.

105

For the top of the hat, place the headband on top of a sheet of paper towelling (or similar lightweight paper or cloth), any color. Pinch the center of the paper towel and bring it up through the headband. Pinch several other sections until the paper towel is even with the top edge of the headband. Turn over and staple the towel to the headband. Trim off the excess towelling.

For the brim, fold a 12-inch square of construction paper, any color, in half. Cut out a semicircle, beginning and ending at the fold edge. Open to form a circle (Figure 1). Place the

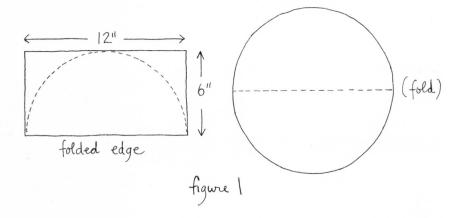

figure 1

headband in the center of the circle. Trace the outline of the outside edge of the headband onto the circle with a pencil. Cut on a straight line to this pencilled circle, and cut it out (Figure 2). This forms an open ring.

Wrap the open ring around the bottom edge of the headband. Overlap the edges so the brim fits snugly, and staple closed. Tape the brim to the headband in several places to keep it firmly attached.

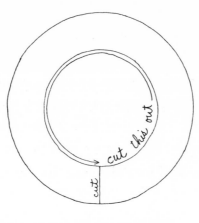

figure 2

☆ plume

Hold two drinking straws side by side and fold in half. Crease the fold ends firmly. Wrap tape around the fold ends to hold the straws together.

Cut a 10-inch long and 2-inch wide strip from a paper towel, tissue paper, ribbon or any other bright-colored, thin material. Fold in half, short sides together. Cut very narrow slits, about 4 inches long, along the side opposite the fold (Figure 3). Pinch the fold end as tightly as possible so it fits into one of the open ends of the straws. Repeat for the other three ends of the straws. If you want a very full plume, use more straws and more fringe.

Stick the taped end of the plume into the groove of the headband on one side of the hat (see costume illustration). Staple in place.

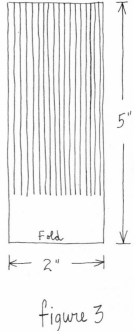

figure 3

107

☆ telescope

Use an empty paper towel tube. Make another tube from paper, at least 1 inch longer and narrow enough to slide inside the paper towel tube. Cover one end of each tube with clear paper or plastic wrap, and tape in place. Place the longer tube inside the paper towel tube so the covered ends are on the outside.

When you are ready to use the telescope, pull out the inside tube about halfway and look through the "glass-covered" end.

Sailor

Extra Quick and Easy

Wear
blue jeans, rolled to the knees
turtleneck T-shirt
long-sleeved shirt, worn over the T-shirt
    with the sleeves rolled to the elbows and
    the tail hanging loose
piece of rope, tied around your waist over
    the shirt
colorful scarf, wrapped around your head
    and tied at the back
sandals
coil of rope, carried over your arm

For standing watch in the crow's nest of the ship, stand in a large bushel basket. Use masking tape to attach a long stick (garden cane, broom handle, volleyball or badminton net pole) to the side of the bushel basket. Cut out a flag shape from paper or fabric scrap. Print the name of the sailor's ship on the flag: "Nina," "Pinta," or "Santa Maria." Tape the flag to the top of the stick.

Queen Isabella

Queen Isabella of Spain was the only ruler who would help pay for Christopher Columbus' daring plan to sail to the West Indies. She and King Ferdinand released money from the Royal Treasury to outfit three sailing ships for the voyage.

Wear
long dress or fancy nightgown. If you borrow a dress from a larger person, tape the front hem and sleeves to fit you. The back of the dress can trail behind in courtly fashion.
party shoes and socks
necklaces, bracelets, rings—as many as you want to wear

Make
☆ crown
Make a headband (see p. 14) from gold wrapping paper or yellow construction paper.
Break ten pieces of thick spaghetti in

109

half. Glue them inside the groove of the headband, spacing them evenly about 1 inch apart. Add as many additional "gold" spaghetti points around the headband as you wish.

Cut two rectangles, each 6 inches long and 3 inches wide, from yellow construction paper or gold wrapping paper. Glue on sequins, beads, bottle caps, aquarium stones, buttons, or whatever else you have that looks jewel-like. Staple or tape one short side of each rectangle to each side of the headband (see costume illustration).

☆ cape

Make an ankle-length cape (see p. 19) from a fancy bedspread, curtain, towel, or other rich-looking material. Drape over your shoulders and pin closed at the neck with a jewelry pin.

United Nations Day

Peaceful Planet

One of the goals of the United Nations is to promote world peace. The dove and olive branch are often used as symbols for peace.

Wear
everyday clothes

Make

☆ world peace sign
Make a sandwich sign (see p. 22) from stiff paper, any color. Trim so the two sign pieces are large globe shapes, between 1 and 2 feet across.

Decorate one sign with pictures of flags, names of countries, scenery and people from around the world. Magazines and the travel section of a newspaper are good sources for pictures and large letters. Also use pictures from brochures from airlines, travel agencies, and tourist board offices.

Decorate the second sign with a United Nations Day message, such as "Peace, United Nations Day, October 24, 19—," or your own U.N. Day message.

☆ dove headdress
Make a headband and one crosspiece (see

p. 14) from white paper. Staple fresh bay leaves, parsley, carrot tops, or spinach leaves all around the headband for olive leaves.

Make the dove from two white letter envelopes, each about 6½ inches long and 3½ inches wide. Fold one envelope in half, long sides together and with the gummed flap on the inside. Fold the long edges inward so they meet at the center crease (Figure 1). Glue the long edges together.

Fold the second envelope in half, short sides together and with the gummed flap on the inside.

Place the first envelope inside the second so the fold edges touch. Center the long envelope so the ends are the same size. Staple the envelopes together near the center of the outside fold edge (Figure 2).

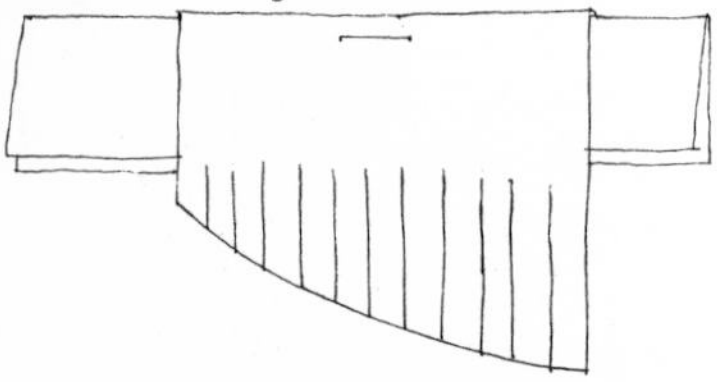

Trim each half of the outside envelope to form the dove's wings. Make slits along each wing side for the bird's feathers (Figure 3).

Cut slits about 1 inch long along one end of the inside envelope for the tail feathers. On the opposite end, cut a beak shape and draw eyes for each side of the head (Figure 4).

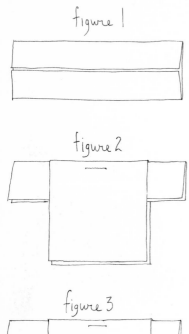

figure 1

figure 2

figure 3

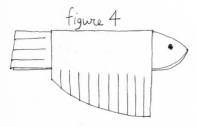

figure 4

Spread the wings and glue the dove to
the crosspiece of the headband.

United Nations Blend

*Wear parts of folk costumes from different countries of the
world. You can wear the items suggested here, or perhaps you
have clothing and accessories of your own which are typical
of those worn in other lands (such as clogs, a beret, or an em-
broidered shirt).*

Wear
cowboy-style shirt from the United States
dark knee-high boots from Russia

Carry
☆ a basket filled with foods from around the
    world:
loaf of bread from France
sauerkraut from Germany
cheddar cheese from England
figs from Egypt
rice or bean sprouts from China
pasta from Italy
curry from India
tortillas from Mexico
olives from Spain

Make
☆ pleated skirt from Greece
Make a knee-length skirt (see p. 17) from white paper, such

113

as shelf paper or freezer wrapping paper. Instead of making short pleats, fold the paper so the pleats go all the way to the bottom edge of the skirt. Fasten the open side and waistband closed in the same way as the full skirt. Tie a red scarf around your waist like a sash.

☆ hat from Japan
Cut a 20-inch square from yellow posterboard or similar stiff paper. Fold in half. Cut out a semicircle, beginning and ending at the fold edge.

Fold the semicircle in half and lightly crease the center of the fold edge (Figure 1). Open to full circle.

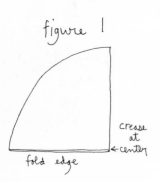

figure 1

crease at ←center

fold edge

Cut along the fold to the creased center. Overlap the cut sides to form a triangular-shaped hat. Staple or tape closed.

The hat fits over your head so your eyes are almost covered. If it is too big, trim the edges to fit, or make another from a slightly smaller square. If you don't have a basket, this hat carried upside down is a good substitute.

Halloween

Monster

While you are putting your monster costume together, practice making monster noises and a spooky, horrible laugh.

Wear
oversized jacket, stuffed (see below)
dark pants
dark T-shirt
oversized gloves, stuffed with paper and
    pinned inside each jacket sleeve
dark shoes and socks

Make
☆ mask

Cut a disposable plastic gallon container (such as milk or juice) in half, with the handle in the center of one side. Use the handle half for the mask.

Place it over your face and mark for eye holes. Cut out the eye holes and, with closed, sharp-pointed scissors, make a hole on opposite edges of the mask level with the eye holes (see Figure 1). Thread a 15-inch piece of string or yarn through each hole, and knot to hold.

Wrap a ball of yarn or string, any color, lengthwise around a thin book about 10 inches long. Make about thirty circles around the book; then clip the yarn at both edges, forming sixty 10-inch strips.

Tape about fifteen yarn strips to the top edge of the face mask and on both sides just above the string ties. Knot the remaining "hair" to the mask ties. Attach the hair so it has many lengths and looks quite wild (Figure 1).

Tie the mask on at the back of your head.

figure 1

☆ monster shoes

With soap and water, clean two medium-sized (7 oz.) tuna fish cans (or similar short, wide cans), each with one lid removed. If you have large feet, clean four cans, two for each foot. Hammer down any sharp edges.

Lid-side upward, poke a hole on opposite sides of each lid with a bottle opener. Thread strong string or polyester yarn,

116

35 inches long, down through one hole and up through the hole on the opposite side. Repeat for the second can.

With your shoes on, place a can under each foot. Ends even, cross the strings over the top of your foot, in back of your ankle, and then tie firmly in the front of your ankle (see costume illustration). (If you are using two cans, place the second can under the toe-end of your shoes and tie the strings on top each shoe. Use a shorter piece of string or yarn for this can.) Practice lifting your feet as you walk—it's easier that way.

☆ chain

Fold a piece of aluminum foil, 12 inches long and 8 inches wide, lengthwise in half. Fold in half two more times in the same way. Fold this strip in half, short sides together. Staple the short end opposite the fold closed. Bring the short ends together to make a ring. Overlap the ends and staple closed.

Repeat, threading the second foil strip through the first foil ring before stapling closed. Continue until your chain is about 18 inches long. The chain hangs in front of the jacket, with the ends taped inside the front pockets.

You can make an even quicker chain by clipping extra-large paper clips to each other, or by using curtain rings in the same way.

☆ shoulder padding for the jacket

Stuff balls of crushed newspaper inside two plastic or paper bags. Tape, staple, or baggie tie the bags closed. Fasten one bag inside the coat at each shoulder with tape or pins.

Or use your own or borrowed football pads.

117

Bat

Wear

long-sleeved, dark T-shirt
dark pants or tights
dark, heavy socks
dark shoes

Make

☆ wings

Cut off the closed, short end from a large, black plastic trash bag. If the fold edges open to form a circular or four-sided bag, staple all along one fold edge to close.

Measure the distance from your neck to your feet. Mark this figure along the closed fold edge.

Extend one arm, and ask a friend to measure the distance from your neck to your wrist. Mark this measurement on either open end of the bag, measuring from the marked fold edge (see Figure 1).

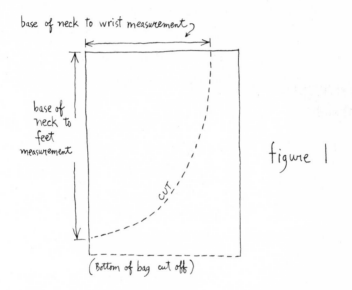

figure 1

Cut out a curve connecting these two points (Figure 1). Open to form the wings (Figure 2).

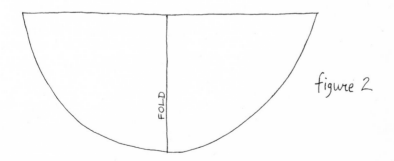

figure 2

119

Extend both arms, and ask a friend to tape the straight edge of the wings to your wrist, elbows, and back. When the bat wings are in place, they will open and close as you move your arms from side to side.

☆ eye mask

Measure the distance around your head and over your eyes. Cut out a black paper strip which is 1 inch longer than this measurement and 2 inches wide. Overlap the short ends of this strip 1 inch, and staple closed.

Put the strip on over your eyes, and carefully mark the eye holes. Cut out the eye holes, and shape the top and bottom edges of the mask to look more bat-like (Figure 3).

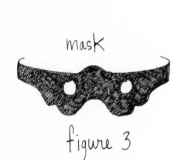

mask

figure 3

☆ ears

Fold a 4-inch square diagonally in half. Cut along the fold to form two triangles. For each triangle, fold in the two corners of the long side so they meet in the center (Figure 4). Crease the folds and staple the shape closed. Staple the bat ears to the side of the eye mask.

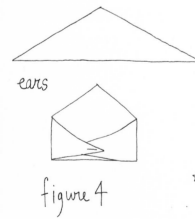

ears

figure 4

☆ fangs

Cut out a rectangle, 2½ inches long, and 1½ inches wide, from a wax carton (such as cottage cheese). Cut one long side so it

120

has a point on each end (Figure 5). Put
the uncut long side between your teeth to
hold the fangs in place.

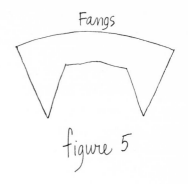

figure 5

Sorcerer

Wear
long-sleeved, dark T-shirt
long, dark pants
boots, any color

121

Make

☆ tunic

Make an ankle-length tunic (see p. 15) from dark cloth or paper. Or use two dark, long skirts, borrowed from someone taller than yourself. Lay flat, one on top of the other, and pin or tape the sides together, except for arm holes near the waistband. Pin or tape the waistbands together, leaving enough room for your head to slide through.

To decorate, cut large diamond shapes from blue paper. Draw or glue a shiny star in the center of each shape. Fasten at least six diamonds to both sides of the tunic with tape, glue, or staples.

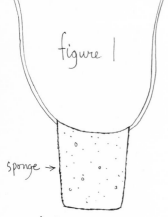

figure 1

sponge →

☆ beard

Cut narrow white ribbon, crepe paper, or yarn so it is long enough to tuck under your chin, and tie on top of your head.

Trim a clean, white sponge to a narrow beard shape (Figure 1), and glue or tape to the middle of the long strip. Tie the beard on your chin before you put on the hat.

☆ hat

Make an extra-thick headband (see p. 14) from 12-inch wide blue construction paper (tape several sheets together, if necessary). Trim to the proper length for your head size, then fold in half three times, long sides together. Overlap the short ends of the strip 1 inch, and staple the headband closed.

Use an empty, medium-sized, rectangular cereal box or

powdered milk box. Cut off the flaps from the open end, and cut off the back of the box. Staple the open end and sides of the box to the front of the headband (see Figure 2). Cover the front and three sides of the box with blue paper.

Flatten a toilet paper tube, or section cut from a paper towel tube. Glue to the center of the top edge of the box. Wrap aluminum foil or any shiny paper around the flattened tube to cover.

Decorate the front of the hat with pictures of the sun, moon, and stars, cut from old magazines; or draw your own. If you have them, use gummed stars, too.

☆ hair

Use several layers of white tissue paper, paper tissues, or paper towels, folded to a length of about 5 inches. Make enough "hair" to cover the sides and back of your head. Staple the "hair" to the headband along the edge opposite the fold (Figure 2).

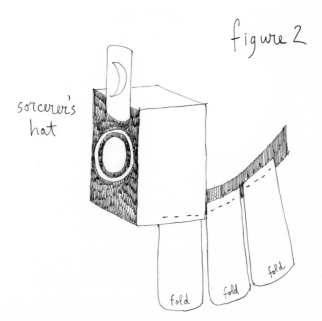

figure 2

sorcerer's hat

fold fold fold

☆ magic wand

Cut out a crescent moon shape from orange, yellow, or white posterboard, which is about 22 inches long and 14 inches wide.

Stack three large sheets of newspaper, one on top the other. Fold in half along the center crease of the newspaper. Beginning at the fold edge, roll the newspaper into a tight tube. Tape closed in several places. Tape the stick to one side of the paper moon, leaving enough space to use as a handle. Cover the handle with dark blue paper or foil wrapping paper.

Ghost

Extra Quick and Easy

Wear
long-sleeved, white T-shirt
long pants (light-colored, if possible)
white socks and sneakers

Make

☆ coverall

Drape an old white sheet, blanket, tablecloth (paper or fabric), or towel over your head. Ask a friend to help mark for eye, nose, and arm holes. Take the sheet off and cut out the holes. Put the sheet on once more and have a friend trim the bottom edge so it just clears the floor.

☆ noisy necklace

Collect a variety of foil pie plates, lids, and containers. With a long, thick nail, carefully poke a hole near the edge of each piece.

Thread a short piece of string or yarn through each hole. Add a few paperclips, bells, or pasta circles; then knot the string to form a circle.

Hang the string circles on a second piece of yarn or string, long enough to tie around your neck.

You might pin additional noisemakers to your coverall, or make another necklace to tie around your waist. Make a long, low "oooooooooooooooo" sound for an additional scary effect.

November

Thanksgiving Day

Pilgrim Man

Wear

dark pants

long-sleeved, dark flannel shirt

dark knee-high boots, worn over your pant legs

dark towel, worn lengthwise across your back like a cape

Make

☆ hat

For the top of the hat, cut a rectangle 4 inches wide and 1 inch longer than your head size from dark-colored construction paper. Bring the short sides together, overlapping the ends 2 inches at one edge and 1 inch at the other. Staple or tape closed. The narrower end is the top edge of the hat.

For the brim, fold a 12-inch square of construction paper (the same color as the top of the hat) in half. Cut out a large semicircle, beginning and ending at the fold edge. Open to form a circle (Figure 1).

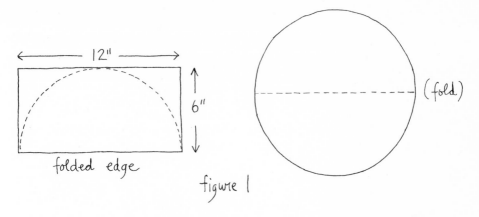

folded edge

12"

6"

(fold)

figure 1

Place the bottom edge of the hat-top in the center of the circle. Trace the shape of the hat onto the circle with a pencil.

Cut on a straight line to the pencilled circle, and cut it out. This forms an open ring (Figure 2). Wrap the open ring around the bottom edge of the hat. Overlap the ends of the ring so it fits the hat-top snugly. Staple closed. Tape the brim to the hat-top to hold firmly in place.

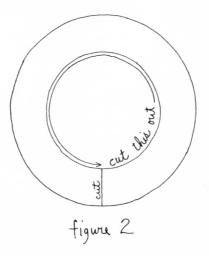

cut this out

figure 2

☆ collar

Fold a 12-inch square of white cloth or paper in half. Fold in half again by bringing the short sides together. Crease the fold edges and open so the square is folded just once.

For the neck opening, mark two points along the fold edge, each 2 inches from the creased center (Figure 3). Make a mark on the creased center, 1 inch down from the fold edge. Draw a curve joining these three marks and cut it out, cutting through both layers of cloth or paper. Then cut along the creased center from the neck opening to the opposite side, cutting only one layer of cloth or paper. The uncut side is the back and the cut side is the front of the collar.

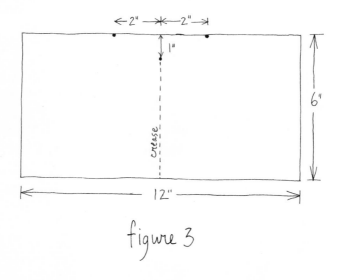

figure 3

Make two small holes in the collar front, one on each side of the center cut and just below the neck opening (Figure 4). If you are making the collar from paper, place a small piece of tape over each hole before you cut or hole punch.

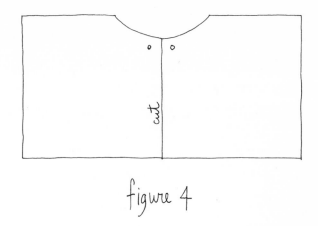

figure 4

Thread a short piece of string or yarn through each hole. Knot or tape to hold. Wear the collar over the cape.

Pilgrim Woman

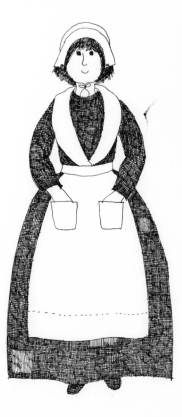

Wear

long-sleeved blouse (or T-shirt) and long
    skirt, or long, colorful dress. Tape sev-
    eral fabric or paper patches on the skirt.
school shoes and socks
long apron (perhaps borrowed from some-
    one larger than yourself)

Make

☆ collar

Tape together or fold white paper napkins, paper towels, paper placemats, a dish
towel, or a pillowcase to form a shape
about 18 inches long and 8 inches wide.
Fold this shape in half, long sides to-

129

gether. Wrap around the back of your neck and overlap the ends at your waist. Fasten the ends with a safety pin or tape, and cover with the apron waistband.

☆ hat
Use any color cloth or paper, 9 inches wide and as long as the distance over the top of your head, measuring from ear lobe to ear lobe.

Make a 2-inch fold along one long side. Crease the fold edge firmly. With a hole punch, make a hole through both layers of cloth or paper near each end of the fold (Figure 1). Thread a

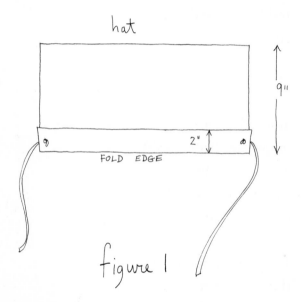

figure 1

10-inch long piece of yarn or string through each hole and knot to hold. Put the hat on your head, fold side outward, and tie the yarn under your chin. If the back of the hat is too long, trim so it is even with the back of your head.

Chief Massasoit

Chief Massasoit, a Wampanoag Indian, made a treaty of friendship with the Pilgrims soon after they landed at Plymouth. He was an honored guest of the Plymouth Pilgrims at their first Thanksgiving celebration.

Wear

tan or brown long pants
long-sleeved, tan or brown shirt or T-shirt
ankle-high socks
small blanket or towel, worn around your
    shoulders and held closed in front with
    a large safety pin

Make

☆ breechcloth

Cut two rectangles from a grocery bag or other brown paper or cloth. Each is as wide as your waist across the front, and as long as the measurement from your waist to slightly above your knees (see costume illustration).

Make small cuts along the bottom edge to look like fringe. Draw a design on one side of each rectangle with crayon or Magic Marker. Tuck the side opposite the fringe into your pants top with the design facing outward. One cloth is for the front, and one for the back.

131

☆ moccasins

Use two brown paper bags large enough to go over your stockinged feet. Tie a piece of yarn around the top of each bag and over your ankle (or use a large rubber band) to keep the moccasins in place.

☆ hair crest

Make a headband (see p. 14) from brown paper or a grocery bag.

figure 1

hair crest

Cut a 4-inch wide crosspiece from brown or black paper. Fold in half, long sides together. Cut slits about ½ inch apart and 1½ inches long along both long sides. Leave a short uncut section at both ends for gluing into the groove of the headband. Crease the fringed portion so the "hair" stands upright, and glue the ends of the strip into opposite sides of the headband (Figure 1).

☆ eagle feather

Cut a large feather shape from the lid of a styrofoam egg carton or large meat container. Stick toothpicks along both long edges. Staple the feather to the back of the headband so it stands upright (see costume illustration).

December

Christmas

Mary

Extra Quick and Easy

Wear
long-sleeved winter nightgown, any color
sandals
old sheet, blanket, afghan, or large shawl,
   long enough to drape over your head
   and shoulders and reach near the floor
carry a doll wrapped in a small blanket

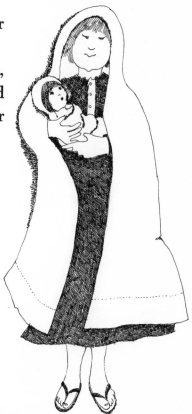

Joseph

Wear

long-sleeved shirt or T-shirt and long
    pants, any color

sandals

small blanket, shawl, or hand towel, worn
    lengthwise over your head and pinned
    closed behind the beard

carry a small knapsack, paper bag, or pil-
    lowcase, stuffed with crushed news-
    paper

Make

☆ tunic

Make an ankle-length tunic (see p. 15)
from green, blue, or brown cloth or paper.
Run strips of wide masking tape from the
neck hole and shoulders to the bottom
edge, spacing them equally all around, to
make the stripes.

☆ beard

From a brown paper bag, cut a rectangle 6 inches long and as
wide as the distance from one ear to the other, measuring across
your chin. Cut a curved beard shape, beginning and ending at
one long side. Stick a small, flesh-colored bandaid at each end
of the straight side. Peel only one-half of each bandaid, so the
other half can be used to hold the beard to your face (Figure 1).

Cover the bandaids and brown paper base with 6-inch pieces
of brown yarn glued in place.

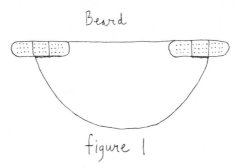

Beard

figure 1

Place the long edge of the beard so it covers your chin and angles upward on your cheeks. Hold in place at the side of your face with the other half of the bandaid strips.

Shepherd's Lamb

Wear

grey or white knit pajamas
white socks, over your hands and feet
large white towel or bathmat,
    worn over your back
    when you are on all fours.
    Pin a 3-inch piece of rope
    or yarn to the back of the towel
    for a tail.

Make

☆ headdress

Cut a 7-inch section from the sleeve of a large white undershirt. Pull the piece over your head and ears like a cap. With a pencil, make a mark at the top of your ears on each side of the undershirt cap.

135

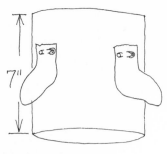

figure 1

For the lamb's ears, use an old pair of small-sized white socks. Stuff the toe end of each sock with crushed paper. Use a large safety pin to fasten each ear to the marked places on the headdress (Figure 1). If necessary, cut off the open end of each sock to make the ears short enough.

Shepherd

Extra Quick and Easy

Wear

long pants, any color

sandals

oversized striped shirt or pajama top, worn outside the pants. Hold the cuffs in place at your wrist with rubber bands.

piece of rope around your waist

large handkerchief, centered on the top of your head so the front edge covers your forehead. Tie a piece of string or yarn around your head just above your eyebrows to hold the handkerchief in place.

furry coat or furry-lined coat turned inside out, worn like a cape. Hold closed at your neck with a large safety pin.

carry a stick, or mop or broom handle for a staff

King I

Wear

long-sleeved T-shirt and long pants, any
color (or leotard and tights)

sandals

ankle-length, long-sleeved fancy bathrobe. If borrowed from someone larger
than yourself, tuck under and tape the
bottom hem, and shorten the sleeves by
tucking them under and holding in
place with rubber bands.

jewelry chain, colorful sash, or belt tied
around your waist and over the robe

carry cloves, perfumed soap, orange peels
or any scented material in a pretty container (such as a gift box, jewelry case,
powder box, or small cookie tin) for the
gift of frankincense

Make

☆ cape

Cut at least ten foil Christmas-tree ropes, long enough to reach
from your neck to your ankle. Tape one end of each foil rope
to a piece of ribbon, long enough to tie around your neck. Be
sure to leave several inches without decoration at each end of
the ribbon, so you can tie it easily. Add additional foil ropes, if
you wish, to make a fuller cape. Tie it on around your neck.

☆ crown

Make a headband (see p. 14) from foil wrapping paper.

137

From red or purple construction paper, make four cross-pieces, each 20 inches long and 2 inches wide. Insert the crosspieces in the groove of the headband, spacing them evenly all around (see costume illustration). Glue or staple in place; then staple the groove closed. Tape the crosspieces together where they meet at the top of the crown.

Glue on Christmas candies, nuts, raisins, popcorn, bits of shiny paper or tinsel to decorate the crosspieces.

King II

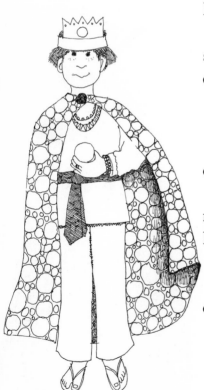

Wear

long-sleeved T-shirt and long pants, any
    color (or leotard and tights)
sandals
oversized silky or satiny shirt, borrowed
    from someone larger than yourself.
    Roll up or tuck under the shirt sleeves,
    and keep in place with rubber bands.
colorful scarf, sash, or man's tie worn
    around your waist and over the shirt
necklaces, rings, bracelets
large fancy skirt, draped over your shoul-
    ders like a double-thickness cape and
    held closed in front with a jewelry pin
carry a gold Christmas ornament, gold
    candy box, or gold foil-covered object
    for the gift of gold

Make

☆ crown

Make a headband (see p. 14) from purple or blue construction paper.

Staple a clean, white styrofoam meat container, about 7 inches long and 5 inches wide, to the front of the headband with the curved edges facing inward. Cut points along the top edge of the container. Decorate the side of the container facing forward with items such as paper fasteners, pushpins, small pieces of crayon, sunflower seeds, paper clips, cloves, jacks, colored toothpicks and similar objects that can be stuck directly into the styrofoam.

King III

Wear

long-sleeved T-shirt and long pants, any
    color (or leotard and tights)
sandals
fancy tablecloth or shower curtain, worn
    as an ankle-length cape. Hold closed
    in front with a jewelry pin.
carry a small bottle of perfume or any
    fancy container (such as soap or bubble
    bath) for the gift of myrrh

Make

☆ tunic

Use two large sheets of shiny gift-wrapping

139

paper, each as long as your measurement from neck to ankle and as wide as your shoulders. One sheet is for the front of the tunic and one is for the back. Ask someone to help you tape the sheets together at the short edge at your shoulders and along the sides.

☆ belt

Cut a piece of cloth (any color) 4 inches wide and long enough to tie around your waist. Glue on short strands of colorful yarn or ribbon, or buttons. Tie the belt around your waist over the tunic, and knot at the side.

☆ crown

Use a paper paint bucket or plastic flower pot, both available from a hardware or variety store. Be sure the open end fits on the top of your head like a hat. Wrap a strand of Christmas tree beads around the sides and bottom of the bucket or flower pot. Put a drop of glue here and there to hold the beads in place. Glue a large Christmas tree bulb to the top of the crown.

Santa Claus

Wear

large-sized, long-sleeved, red T-shirt or flannel shirt

large-sized, red pants or pajama bottoms. Tuck a pillow inside the waistband.

black knee-high boots, worn over the pant legs

old pillowcase or knapsack, stuffed with toys, candy, empty gift boxes, or crushed paper to look like Santa's pack

140

Make

☆ cap

Cut a 12-inch long section from the narrow end of the sleeve from an old, red knit T-shirt, or from a sleeve or pant leg from red knit pajamas. Slide the wider end of this section over your head like a cap to make sure it fits snugly. Remove and turn inside out.

Staple the smaller open end to form a point, and turn right side out again. Stuff the pointed end with a small ball of paper or cloth. Staple cotton balls all around the open end of the cap and one at the tip of the point.

☆ beard

Cut a piece of white paper or old sheet, 6 inches long and as wide as the distance from one ear to the other, measuring under your nose. Trim one long side to form the bottom edge of the beard.

On the long, straight side, cut a hole 1 inch down from the center for the mouth hole.

Put small pieces of tape in each corner of the top edge of the beard. With a hole punch, make a hole through each taped part. Thread a 15-inch long piece of string or yarn through each hole, and knot onto the beard at one end.

Glue white cotton balls or small pieces of rolled cotton to cover the paper or fabric. Add small cotton balls or a narrow, tube-shaped section of cotton above the mouth hole to form Santa's moustache.

141

Tie the beard on at the back of your head, then slide the cap over your head to cover the string or yarn ties.

☆ buckle and belt

Cut a rectangle 4 inches long and 2½ inches wide from cardboard, such as an empty tissue box or department store box. Fold in half, short sides together. Cut out a 1½-inch square in the center of the fold edge (Figure 1). Open to form an open rectangle.

Cut two 1-inch wide strips from aluminum foil, each about 12 inches long. Wrap the strips around the four sides of the cardboard rectangle to cover.

Cut a 2-inch wide strip from aluminum foil, about 12 inches long. Fold in half twice, long sides together, to form a long narrow strip. Wrap around the foil-covered rectangle at the center of the long sides to make the center bar of the belt (Figure 2). Staple to hold in place.

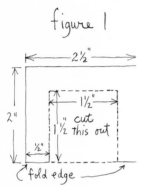

figure 1

2½"

2"

1½"

½" cut
1½ this out

½"

fold edge

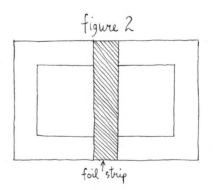

figure 2

foil strip

Cut a 1-inch wide piece of dark cloth or paper, 6 inches longer than your waist measurement (or long enough to wrap around your pillow-stuffed waist) for the belt. Staple one short end to a short side of the buckle. Hold the buckle in front of you, and wrap the belt around your waist. Thread the loose end of the belt over the short end of the buckle, under the center bar, and over the opposite short end (Figure 3). Tape to hold.

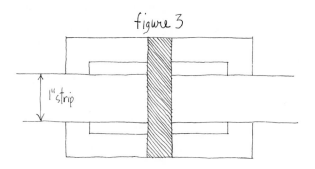

figure 3

1" strip

Chanukah

Judah Maccabeus

In the second century B.C., the leader of the Syrian empire tried to make the Temple of Jerusalem a temple for the Greek religion. Judah Maccabeus led a small group of Jewish men to a surprising victory over a large Syrian army, and re-dedicated the Temple to the Jewish religion.

Wear
long-sleeved T-shirt, any color
shorts
sandals

Make
☆ shield
Carry a garbage can lid, or make a shield
from a large, aluminum foil roasting pan.
To make a handle for the roasting pan,
poke two holes about 4 inches apart in the
center of the pan using closed, sharp-
pointed scissors. Thread a 10-inch piece
of string or yarn through one hole and
knot on the outside of the pan (Figure 1).
Thread the other end through the second
hole and knot in the same way.

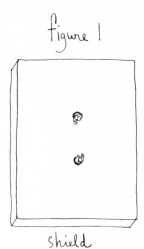

figure 1

shield

☆ tunic
Make a knee-length tunic (see p. 15) from light brown cloth
(such as burlap) or paper cut from a large grocery bag. For
the fringe, make small cuts along the bottom edge about 2
inches long and as close together as possible. Tie a dark scarf,
strip of cloth, or crepe paper around your waist for a sash.

☆ cape
Make an ankle-length cape (see p. 19) from white, tan, or grey
material, such as a pillowcase, towel, or section from an old
sheet.
    Drape the cape over your shoulders as you would normally
wear it. Then pull one corner over across your chest to the op-

posite shoulder. Hold in place with a large safety pin (see costume illustration).

☆ staff

Use a long stick, or mop or broom handle. Or make one from two large grocery bags. Roll each bag lengthwise into a tight tube, or fold in half three times bringing the long sides together. Tape the thick strip or tube closed in at least four places. Hold end to end to form one long stick, and wrap tape around the center to hold the two pieces together.

Cut a large flag shape from white paper or cloth. With blue Magic Marker draw the Lion of Judah (Figure 2), or a Jewish star. Attach the flag to the top of the staff with tape or glue.

figure 2

146

Menorah

According to Jewish tradition, when the menorah or holy candelabra in the Temple of Jerusalem was lit after the victory over the Syrian Army, it burned for eight days although there was barely enough oil for one day. To celebrate this miracle, Jews light small menorahs in their home—one candle each night until all eight candles are burning. The center candle, called the Shammash *or "servant," is lit each night and is used to light the others.*

Wear
everyday clothes or party clothes

Make
☆ menorah headdress
Make a headband (see p. 14) from gold or silver wrapping paper.

Make the candles from pencils, straws, or crayons. Make the flame from bits of red, yellow, or orange wax from candle drippings or the wax covering from cheese. Soften the wax by rolling it between your fingers, then pinch it over the top of your homemade candles.

Glue the candles into the front groove of the headband, with the larger candle in the center and the eight smaller ones evenly spaced on both sides. Staple the groove closed.

147

☆ sandwich sign

Make a large sandwich sign (see p. 22) from two pieces of colorful construction paper.

Collage both sides with Chanukah wrapping paper, shiny paper, gift package ribbons, Jewish stars (Figure 1), and other festive decorations. With Magic Marker or crayon, print "Happy Chanukah" on one side, and "A Great Miracle Happened There" on the other.

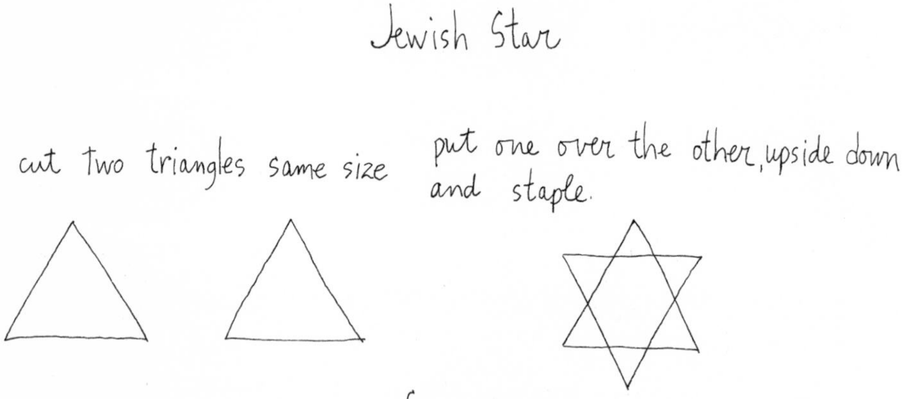

Jewish Star

cut two triangles same size   put one over the other, upside down and staple.

figure 1

Dreydl

A dreydl is a four-sided top used on Chanukah to play a game of chance. Players win or lose nuts, candy, pennies, or other small items depending upon which Hebrew letter they spin on the dreydl. Nun *stands for the Hebrew word meaning "nothing";* gimel *stands for "all";* hay *stands for "half"; and* shin *for "add" or "put in." These letters are also the first letters of the words meaning "a great miracle happened there," which refers to the eight-day burning of the oil in the Temple menorah.*

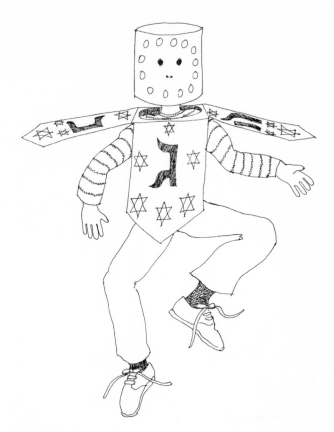

Wear
everyday clothes

Make
☆ dreydl

Cut a 12-inch square from brightly-colored posterboard or stiff cardboard. Cut out a circle in the center of the square large enough for your head to pass through.

Cut four rectangles from brightly-colored construction paper, each 18 inches long and 12 inches wide. Cut a large point on a 12-inch side of each piece. On the side opposite the point, make a 1-inch wide crease.

Print a different Hebrew letter on one side of each pointed

149

piece (Figure 1). Decorate the rest of the construction paper with Jewish stars (see *Menorah,* p. 148), Chanukah wrapping paper, or other holiday symbols.

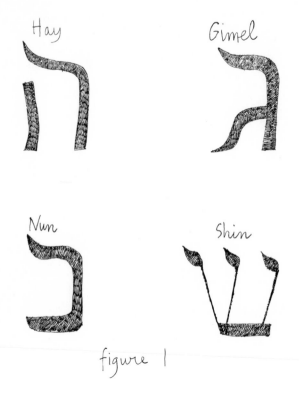

Hay

Gimel

Nun

Shin

figure 1

Staple, tape, or glue each creased edge of the lettered pieces to an edge on the 12-inch square.

☆ dreydl spinner
Cut a large rectangle from a paper bag or construction paper, large enough to wrap around your head and cover your face. Roll the paper so it fits over your head like a tube and tape

closed. With a pencil, carefully mark for eye and nose holes. Remove the tube and cut out the marked points.

Decorate the tube with real or paper pennies, candy, raisins, nuts, dried cereal, or other treats. The tube is the spinner for the dreydl.

Index

About the Author

Vivienne Eisner was born in Dayton, Ohio and graduated from George Washington University and Southern Connecticut State College, where she received a master's degree in Art Education. As an art instructor, she has taught elementary school children, parents, and teachers. The mother of three grown children, Ms. Eisner lives in Teaneck, New Jersey, where she devotes full-time to writing books for children and adults.